STATE OF BASS

MARTIN JAMES

Martin James is a music and popular culture journalist who contributes to *Muzik, Melody Maker, Sweater* (USA) and *Urb* (USA). He has also contributed to the *Guardian* and currently edits the media and home entertainments sections of *Muzik*.

Martin writes and records music under a variety of guises, DJs regularly and has promoted clubs and raves in the Midlands.

STATE OF BASS

JUNGLE: THE STORY SO FAR

MARTIN JAMES

FOREWORD BY A GUY CALLED GERALD

B■XTREE

First published in 1997 by Boxtree, an imprint of Macmillan Publishers
Ltd, 25 Eccleston Place, London, SW1W 9NF and Basingstoke

Associated companies throughout the world

ISBN 07522 23232

9 8 7 6 5 4 3 2 1

A CIP catalogue record for this book is available from the British Library

Cover design by Blackjacks

Typeset by SX Composing DTP, Rayleigh, Essex
Printed by Mackays of Chatham plc, Chatham, Kent

SHOUTS TO:

For their enthusiasm, encouragement and support, I'd like to give a huge thanks to: Lisa Jayne, James Hyman (MTV), Jake Lingwood, Jenny Olivier, Tim Barr, Mark Spivey, Sally and Harvey (Zzonked), Eddie, The Reinforced Crew (Dego, Mark, Gus and Ian), Marc Royal, Dave, Vini, Lisa and the rest of the SOUR Posse, Veena Verdi, James and Andy (Formula), Craig at Juicebox, Zoe (PM Scientists), Cristian, Kemistry and Storm, Colin Steven (Knowledge), Laurence (Electric), Rob Playford, Carl Loben, Sherman, Steve at Island, Push, Andrew Chetty and all of those who agreed to be interviewed.

Also a special thanks to all of my family and friends for their belief and support over the last few months and to A Guy Called Gerald for his foreword.

To Tansey and the bump

CONTENTS

GLOSSARY OF TERMS   ix

FOREWORD   xii

INTRODUCTION
Here Comes the Drumz   xiii

1 ALLA THE JUNGLIST
Naming the Sound   1

2 SHUT UP AND DANCE
Creating the Space for Jungle   5

3 VALLEY OF THE SHADOWS
The Media Blackout and the Rise of Dark   18

4 ARMED AND DANGEROUS
Ragga Jungle Takes Control   32

5 ABOVE THE LAW
The Business Infrastructure   48

6 SHADOW BOXING
The Jungle/Drum 'n' Bass Split   55

7 INTELLIGENT MINDS OF JUNGLE
The Rise of Ambient Drum 'n' Bass   71

8 FEEL THE SUNSHINE
Taking on the Mainstream   83

9 MUTANT REVISITED
Drum 'n' Bass Returns to the Darkside   99

10 THE WORLD IS A GHETTO
Celebrity, the International Growth of Drum 'n' Bass and the
  Jump Up Reaction   109

11 AQUARIUS RISING
The Future   127

SOURCE MATERIAL   131

GLOSSARY OF TERMS

At the risk of patronising those who already know about Jungle, I've included a list of terms which crop up throughout *State of Bass* to assist anyone who is new to the sound.

AMBIENT DRUM 'N' BASS

A very smooth style which uses a wash of dreamy string sounds combined with timestretched breakbeats. Also known as Artcore.

BALEARIC

Eclectic mix of music which provided the soundtrack for Ecstasy parties in Ibiza in the late 1980s.

THE BREAK

Named after the record or artist which supplied the source material. The most popular breaks are Amen (taken from an Amen Brothers track) and Apache (from an updated version of The Shadows' 'Apache'). Those whose origins are less clear include Paris, Cool is Back, Soul Pride and the Scotty Break, which was previously known as Psychic.

THE BREAKBEAT

A rhythmical pattern created by stretching short musical passages or 'breaks' in records. This is achieved either by playing identical records on two decks and switching from one to the other to create a continuous extended passage, or by digitally encoding the 'break' with a sampler and then repeating the pattern in a continuous sequence, or 'loop'.

DARK

The interim sound between Hardcore and Jungle which employed disorientating Ambience, horror film samples and timestretched breakbeats. Also called Darkcore and Horrorcore.

DRUM 'N' BASS

Pre-1994 a term used to describe the basic element of Jungle. Post-1994, the term is used to describe a more musical and technologically complex strain of Jungle.

HARDSTEP

A minimal form of Jungle which strips away much of the melody and uses a cleaner breakbeat, with added treble to exaggerate the crispness of sound. The breakbeats usually emphasise the second and the fourth beats.

HARDCORE

A harder and faster derivative of Hip House circa 1990–91 which uses a combination of sped up breakbeats lifted from Hip Hop and Belgian Techno. Usually typified by staccato melody, high pitched vocals and a regular 4/4 beat bass drum. Also known as Rave music.

HIP HOUSE

A combination of Hip Hop breakbeats and Chicago House which was popular towards the end of 1989 and through the following year.

JAZZ STEP

Hardstep laced with occasional Jazz refrains.

JAZZY JUNGLE

Ambient Drum 'n' Bass with jazzy refrains added. Usually derived from 1980s Jazz Funk records.

JUMP UP

Closely related to the original Jungle form but with extra emphasis on the Hip Hop influence.

JUNGLE

The generic term for all versions of the sound. A combination of timestretched breakbeats playing at approximately 160 beats per minute (bpm) with bass lines lifted from Reggae, running at 80 bpm and the metronomic 4/4 bass drum removed.

RAGGA

A form of Reggae which features vocals rapped or 'chatted' by an MC (microphone controller) over instrumental versions of the music. The lyrics comprise a raw marriage of Jamaican patois and the street slang of inner city London.

RAGGA-JUNGLE

The combination of Ragga's vocal lines ('licks') and Jungle's rhythms.

RAVE

Term used to describe large scale dance events. Also a generic term for the music associated with the events, i.e. Hip House and Hardcore.

SLENG TENG

A fusion between Reggae and the European Techno sound of Kraftwerk which is defined by its buzzing bass line.

TECHSTEP

Similar to Hardstep but with the emphasis on a metallic sound and an undercurrent of menacing noises. Also typified by its extremely loud, distorted bass line which usually uses a maximum of three notes with the octaves emphasised.

TIMESTRETCHING

A technological device which allows you to alter the tempo of a sample without changing the pitch.

FOREWORD

we have reached what could be
the final stage in musical change this century
but it is still in its early days
this music takes on many forms
breaks through many boundaries
I hear it in everything
but what does this mean to the rest of the
all seeing non listening world
f**k all
but even this has a positive role to play
for the mass ignorance of joe public
reflects the brain washing society
we have come to call modern life
in fact
if an individual seeks enlightenment
he or she is often classed as a
nutter
space baby
freak
weirdo
by the mass body of brainless sheep
these patterns echo through the behaviour
of all of our so-called civil societies
put all this aside
there's one way of communicating
of breaking through prejudice
. . . MUSIC

GCG

(A Guy Called Gerald)

INTRODUCTION

HERE COMES THE DRUMZ

The summer of 1996. Standing in the surreal surroundings of Barcelona's Cactus Garden, John Coxon of East End Drum 'n' Bass duo Spring Heel Jack mulls over the continuing worldwide growth of the Junglist sound. It comes as no surprise to him that the power of Drum 'n' Bass has proved to be Britain's most seductive musical export in almost twenty years. What does surprise him, however, is the overwhelming need people have to trace the history of the scene. 'This music is all about moving forwards' he exclaims. 'This is why it constantly changes without people even realising it. Definitive history just isn't as important as what's immediately ahead but people like journalists are always trying to trace its history. It's just not as important as the music itself.'

In many ways Coxon's claim is true. At its finest, Jungle has been all about forgoing standardisation in favour of the sonic experiment. From the extreme approach to sampling and chopping the breaks to the sci-fi ambience of much of the melody, the scene has long held a fascination with existing on electronica's outside edge. This disregard of the given system is a trademark of the Junglist mentality. A mentality which is about exploring the frontiers; breaking with traditional barriers in search of a new realm.

However, despite this apparent rejection of history, the historical perspective of the Jungle scene has become paramount to those involved. History is what holds people down to a common cause. A joint history which has been typified by lengthy periods of media disinterest and episodes of major label exploitation. It's the Jungle scene's very real history which provides it with a sense of place. While no one else was interested, a small collection of style renegades kept faithful to the music they loved and in turn presented an image of a family unified against the rest of the world. A family of people 'in the know'.

State of Bass is all about this family, its passion, energy and enthusiasm. Its intrigue and politics and above all its music. From the moment rave was forced back underground to the Jungle raves of the early 1990s. From the birth of Dark in the dingy recesses of a small club in Islington to the worldwide proliferation of Drum 'n' Bass today, the growth of Jungle has been a story of the collective minority forging change through their own unending belief.

To be a Junglist is to live and breathe the scene, the sounds and the style. It's all about being there, a face in the crowd at the clubs and events, nodding with approval as the DJ drops the latest up front dub plate. It's all about a subconscious sharing of that collective knowledge. Which DJs are collaborating with which producers, who's running the latest imprint or club night. Threads of knowledge which tie you into the greater fabric of the family, giving you a sense of belonging.

Today the numbers of people who claim to have been there from the beginning could outsell the biggest raves of 1990. In reality only a few people had a hand in the running of the scene back in the early days. For my own part I acknowledge that I can hardly call myself a face in the scene, either then or now. True, I was an aficionado of the warehouse parties of 1987, an Acid House head in 1988 and a raver through to the end of the decade. But, inspired by the eclecticism of the early sets of many of Jungle's premier DJs, I was also deep into Hip Hop and Funk. Living in the Midlands (Nottingham) during this time I had little access to the pirate stations which championed the Jungle sounds and raves had simply turned into aberrations of their earlier incarnation.

I was never particularly drawn to the progressive House scene which to me seemed like discotheque music for posers. Hardcore had turned into a pre school-age soundtrack and for a while it seemed like lean times lay ahead for fans of Breakbeat House.

One Friday night at a rave in Nottingham's Marcus Garvey Centre the DJ dropped 'Eye Memory' by local boys Nebula II on Reinforced Records. A slice of dark and brooding energy, its breaks seemed to snap at the synapses, sending my already fried brain cells reeling in unadulterated frenzy. One tune which led me straight to the local record shop on a mission for more. Whether I was late with this new discovery or totally on it was irrelevant. The simple fact was this: the flame of the vibe had been rekindled in me and now I was stepping into the fire of the unknown.

That first record shopping session immediately unearthed a gem. 'Terminator' by Metalheads, again on Reinforced. A tune that I later discovered was produced by Goldie, it seemed to me to be the most perfect slice of genuflected chaos I'd ever experienced. A cut and shut masterpiece which directed me straight on to that path marked 'Dark'.

But this book isn't about me or my perspectives on the scene. The simple matter of the fact is that, although I had a passion for the music I never went to A.W.O.L. at The Paradise Club. Jungle, Dark, Drum 'n' Bass, call it what you will, may have provided a major part of the soundtrack to my life but I was never a part of the London scene.

State of Bass is a story based upon the myriad truths, views and theories drawn from thoughts expressed by those few who experienced things from the very beginning and many others who joined the party later down the line. This is by no account a definitive history of the scene, neither is it a biography of certain individuals elevated to celebrity status over the years. It's simply a version of events culled from the multiple versions already aired. In the great tradition of the version *State of Bass* is a remix or a dub plate for future remodelling.

And in a sense I am, with respect to the MC of the same name, a navigator guiding the reader through the matted vines and tangled roots of the phenomenon known as . . . Jungle.

1: ALLA THE JUNGLIST

NAMING THE SOUND

It always has been such a terrible name. I've never known any other type of music to get so misconstrued by its name.

Rob Playford

Of all the dance music subcultures none have been surrounded with quite so much controversy over its generic term as Jungle. No sooner had it been coined than exponents of the scene were up in arms about Jungle's racist implications. Arguments raged over who first coined the term and many others simply refused to acknowledge Jungle's existence.

The first record to be released using the term Jungle was released by Ibiza. A white label attributed to Johnny Jungle (aka High Wycombe's Pascal of the Ganja Kru), it embraced all of the musical concerns of the scene at the time (breakneck beats coupled with half time b-lines) and quickly became a club favourite. However, as to whether this was the first time the term was used was another matter.

A number of different versions of the origination of the name exist. In Jonathan Fleming's book *What Kind of House Party is This?*, Jason Kyriakides of Hardcore outfit Top Buzz laid claim to the origins of the term: 'We originally said "Jungle Techno" just as a phrase, but people jumped on to it when it wasn't really meant to mean anything. Jungle was just a word to describe the feeling of the music that was being made.'

Although this may well have been a brash claim made in the heat of the moment and taped for posterity, the truth is that it's unlikely that any one individual can lay claim to the term. Just as Hardcore was coined by MCs reacting to the fierce energy they were seeing and hearing, calling up a spontaneous holler of ' 'ardcore massive', then Jungle too will have had similarly intangible beginnings. A word, a feeling in the ether, a sense that what was happening in the lives of British youth was somehow Junglist.

According to MC Navigator, one of the scene's leading MCs and a regular on London's main pirate station, Kool FM, the term 'Jungle' does have a very concrete beginning. The term, he suggests, relates to a sample on a Rebel MC track from '91 – a sample which itself has a far greater cultural significance. 'Rebel got this chant – "alla the junglist" – from a yard-tape (i.e. a soundsystem mix tape from Jamaica),' he explained to the *Melody Maker*'s Simon Reynolds. 'There's a place in Kingston called Tivoli Gardens, and the people call it Jungle. When you hear on a yard-tape the MC sending a big-up to "alla the junglist", they're calling out for the posse from Tivoli. When Rebel sampled that, people cottoned on, and soon they started to call the music "Jungle". I live in Broadwater Farm, a real concrete Jungle, and we called ourselves Junglists long before the music ever came along.'

Such a claim would of course make far more sense than any spurious boast by a Hardcore MC. With much of Jungle's spiritual energy coming from the black Britons of Jamaican descent, the yard-tapes were as much a part of the Jungle aesthetic as soundsystem clashes, dub plates and of course the Ragga samples. Furthermore the term 'Junglist' purveyed a militancy which was quite simply a way of life within the housing estates of Britain's inner cities. The urban jungle.

Whatever the origins, the name was as controversial as the music it represented. For many like DJ Randall, 'it was just the right name for it, it suited it to a tee'. Jungle fit perfectly with life in urban Britain, it encapsulated the concrete Jungle, life on the urban front line where the laws of the Jungle flourished. 'It's a Jungle out there' said Grandmaster Flash in reference to life in the hoods of America on his 1981 cut 'The Message' and here was a generation of British youth was finding it out for themselves.

'There's so much colour in it. So much rhythm. So much texture. You could go into a Jungle and find these things,' reflects A Guy Called Gerald. 'You could sit there in a pool in the middle of a Jungle and there would be flowers, insects, dangerous animals, dangerous plants. But there would be a lot of beautiful sounds. That's one concept of it. Another concept is that the whole society is becoming like a Jungle anyway.'

The term 'Jungle' may have offered a representation of inner city life to some but to many others it was quite simply racist. Often cited as the godfathers of the scene, Shut Up and Dance were quick to denounce 'Jungle' for its racist overtones. 'Jungle' may have had its roots in Jamaica, but in its 1990s context it was more often employed as a racist term against this mainly black form of rave. Indeed 'Jungle' opened up a lot of racist attitudes which had rarely been a feature in the days of Ecstasy fuelled togetherness. Suggesting that it was simply a 'derogatory term', Dave Stone argues that it came from people's bigotry. 'People were going, like, "it's music that the Jungle bunnies dance to" and that I think is how it was coined "Jungle",' says Stone. 'But the people took the word "Jungle" and turned it on its head and made it a positive thing rather than negative. Very much in the same way as the word "nigger" has been reappropriated by the American Hip Hop scene.'

In an interview in *Wax Magazine* (formally known as *Generator*, one of the only dance magazines to support the Hardcore scene), Fabio approaches the race issue from a different angle. Drawing a direct line to the mainly black (and gay) artists of the early days of House music he explains that for him the origins of the name had little to do with life in the urban sprawl, nor was it directly down to Rebel MC's yard-tape sampling. 'What we used to call Jungle was Strictly Rhythm – that was Jungle because it sounded like a load of Jungle percussion sounds, and we used to do House and call it Jungle. So Jungle's coming from that, Nu Groove and fucking Strictly Rhythm . . . we just liked the drums, and a lot of people don't understand – it's not about some fucking Ragga lyrics.'

This view of Jungle is one which is shared by many others in the scene. Mark and Dego of 4 Hero simply refer to it as House music, an extension or reinterpretation of what had gone on before. A sentiment also held by Rob Playford whose view of the scene is in terms of a development in House. 'I still call what we do House music because it's an engineer's thing,' he explains in the Soho offices of his Moving Shadow label. 'It carries on that tradition of House musicians of using down time in studios to create simple dance tracks without vocals. That's the tradition, that's what we do today. And as far as I'm concerned we're always going to be there making the seeds which grow into the next thing. But it's all House music at the end of the day.'

Although many of the formative scene's main players embraced the name readily, many others avoided it with a passion. The use of the term Jungle to describe much of the music produced remains controversial too. To the observer the Breakbeat scene developed from Hardcore and had started to show signs of musical splits from the off. A few years later a split between the Ragga-based Jungle sound and the instrumental form called Drum 'n' Bass became a fully fledged reality. Drum 'n' Bass may have been documented as being the offspring of the increasingly mainstream Ragga-Jungle but there are many who believe that the two were developing side by side, with the emphasis on the term Drum 'n' Bass. The experimental Drum 'n' Bass artist T-Power aka Marc Royal argues:

People used to call a lot of the Breakbeat stuff Drum 'n' Bass. It was because that's what the music had become like, the melody just wasn't as important as the core elements of the rhythm anymore. There were always elements within the Drum 'n' Bass which were 'Junglist'. They were referred to as 'Junglism', but it wasn't Jungle. It was simply Junglism or Drum 'n' Bass. And no one really came out of the other – they were all sort of happening within the same movement. Everyone was feeding off each other and it was as they became genres in their own right that things started to split. Jungle didn't come through as a real genre until 'Dark' had run its course. This was when the Ragga audience got drawn in.

Little surprise then that Goldie refuses to use the term Jungle when describing his music, preferring instead 'inner city Breakbeat'.

Whatever the truth of Jungle's origins, whatever the realities of the implications of the word, by the time the press had cottoned on to the scene they'd universally reported this phenomenon to be called 'Jungle'. And as such the wider public, rightly or wrongly, soon came to accept the genre as Jungle.

2: SHUT UP AND DANCE

CREATING THE SPACE FOR JUNGLE

In 1994 Noah, owner of the seminal imprint Kicking Records, suggested that there was 'actually no such music as Jungle'. In many ways this is true. Jungle itself is a genre which has been tagged with a variety of names and which owes its existence to a myriad of genres. From Dark to Hardstep, Artcore to Drum 'n' Bass; from the appropriation of Reggae and Jazz to the adaptation of Techno and Hip Hop, each new variation on the theme has resulted in a new name to describe the sound. Indeed there are many who still refer to Jungle as Hardcore or breakbeat. In truth, however, all names are correct. Jungle is no one single thing, it's a magpie genre taking from the entire spectrum of music as it sees fit. Indeed many of the scene's players refer to this approach as a '360-degree' thing. Jungle is mercurial. Flowing in all directions, drawing influences from everywhere and inevitably becoming an influence itself.

The liquid nature of the sound is as much to do with the many routes which brought people to the Jungle as it is to do with the technology employed to create the sound. A Rave sound with a street smart attitude, Jungle's early innovators came from Hip Hop backgrounds, b-boys (break-boys) who'd grown tired of Britain's inability to produce a cohesive Hip Hop scene and had started to look to the raves for that unity. Similarly the raves drew on Reggae and Ragga's soundsystem mentality, inspiring the crews to leave the blues parties behind and explore the cybertech vision of the rave.

But Jungle drew on so much more than Rave, Hip Hop and Reggae.

Listen to any number of tracks released over the last six years and you'll hear Soul, R&B, Jazz and of course Techno. Indeed the sound of Drum 'n' Bass is the hybridisation of the last thirty years of technology-based black music.

But when did Jungle first start? And more importantly, what happened to create this stunning marriage of chaotic order and fractured beauty? To understand this you need to look back to Jungle's roots.

ROOTS TO THE JUNGLE

Tracing the roots of Jungle back to a definitive starting point is nigh on impossible. As with most of the technologically enhanced post-Acid House musical developments, Jungle's emergence has had much to do with the influence of sociological, political and economic events outside of the music.

In many ways, however, the seeds of creative force which resulted in the Junglist vision can be found in the dying days of the Ecstasy induced positivity of 1988's Acid House explosion. Often referred to as the Summer of Love, 1988 saw a proliferation in the number of illegal warehouse parties emerging throughout the country. In direct opposition to the overpriced and designer centred legal clubs, warehouse events appealed to individual spontaneity. Venues could be anything from an old abattoir to a disused car park; anywhere which had a power supply and relatively easy access.

Central to the warehouse parties was the relatively recent flood of Ecstasy on to the market. A designer recreational drug, the positivity enhancing Ecstasy (MDMA) provided the user with a new found acceptance of other people and ultimately an enhanced empathy with beats. Ecstasy, the dancing drug went on to fuel a summer of mad spontaneity; an exaggerated version of the 1960s hippy happenings as witnessed through years of television reruns, and now being relived in a modern context.

But the time of the so-called Summer of Love which followed had little to do with the peace, love and understanding ethos of the hippy heyday. This version of events was far more hell bent on a hedonistic lifestyle of dancing in the name of unity till you dropped . . . and then getting up and doing it all over again. Little wonder then that by the close of the year this drug-centred, trespassing party generation had brought upon it a media induced frenzy of outraged attacks. This lifestyle presented a frightening menace which had to be stamped out. And acting as the voice of social morality, the tabloid press instigated a witch hunt against Acid House.

By the much vaunted Second Summer of Love the call to party had become so strong that the back to basics urban warehouse parties slowly became superseded by laser driven spectaculars in the countryside. Inevitably the police responded with a heavy handed attitude of zero tolerance.

Until now the scene had survived on the use of communication technology. Pirate stations would blast out the clues to the locations of the raves, convoys of ravers would congregate at service stations passing on the word. The only information provided on a flyer would be a mobile telephone number with the location of the party not being given out until enough people had phoned in. Eventually there was even a rave line to call, a typically militant appropriation and misuse of BT's voice bank system which allowed numerous lines into a single answering machine. Technology which allowed messages to be changed quickly in order to thwart police attempts to stop the party.

The illegal party spirit slowly became more extreme as organisers became ever more slick in their operations. Rob Playford, who later went on to become one of the most influential people in the Jungle scene, thanks to his Moving Shadow label and his productions, was involved with the Ibiza party organisation at the time. Still holding with the warehouse ethos, in the face of the super raves like Sunrise, the Ibiza team were able to pinpoint a location, move in and turn it round as a venue within a matter of hours. 'It was mad, we'd be straight in there and then it was just like bosh, bosh, bang, the whole thing was ready to roll,' he exclaims. 'We knew it couldn't last but we kept on thinking of more ingenious ways of putting the police off our scent. To start off with they [the police] were pretty crap but towards the end of '89 they started to get their act together and it started to get really difficult.'

Indeed as the warehouse parties flourished the police improved their systems for dealing with this apparent problem. Using unparalleled tactics to stamp out the ravers, Chief Superintendent Ken Tappanden set up a unit to monitor the moves of the ravers and to compile a database of names.

Called the Pay Party Unit, the head office for this operation was in Gravesend, an ideal location to monitor the movements on the M25, which had become the most important road link for the party revellers. In his astonishing book *Altered State*, Matthew Collin details just how seriously the police were taking the rave phenomenon:

Chief Superintendent Ken Tappenden set up the Pay Party Unit with a staff of six and four computers, at a cost of around £100,000. Within a few months there were sixty staff and thirty computers hooked into the HOLMES database, the national police computer network set up in the wake of the Yorkshire Ripper fiasco, and Gravesend had become the party intelligence unit for the whole of England and Wales.

The police had declared war on the ravers and the tactics they had started to employ were frightening in the extreme. Rob Playford recalls the event which was to be his last following a terrifying display of macho from the authorities. Still amazed by what he witnessed, he recalls:

It was supposed to be the third in a series of ten Ibizas. Basically we'd all gone in there really early and beat the police. That was the main thing: to get there before the police because once it was going they couldn't really do much. But then a lot of people got stopped from coming in; cars were being turned back, the drivers and passengers questioned. There was a big task force of police out there but they didn't understand just how much these parties meant to the kids. They'd do anything to get there. We were looking out from the top of this window and all we could see was the police hitting kids who were running across the field. You'd get kids running towards the warehouse and suddenly there was a fist in the face from a copper. Dogs were being set on them and searchlights were being scanned across the fields like it was a war or prison or something. It obviously wasn't a good sight to see. At exactly five a.m. all the windows of the place got smashed in and then rolling through these windows were, like, storm troopers. It was such a frightening sight. They were so over the top, no one made any trouble but they pushed us all into a really tight corner and searched us all. After this we just thought 'this has got beyond a joke now'.

The government's punchline which was finally to turn the rave sour came in July 1990 with Graham Bright's Entertainments (Increased Penalties) Bill. Aimed at the heartland of the illegal rave (or pay party), the Bill raised the maximum fines for unlicensed parties from £2,000 to £20,000 and six months imprisonment. Satellite Pay Party Units were set up throughout the UK and the scene was provided with three choices: defy the law and go back underground; put more effort into promoting special nights in the existing clubs; or apply for licenses to hold legal raves.

YOU KNOW THE SCORE

If the late 1980s cat-and-mouse games between the ravers and the police were centred around London's M25 orbital then the next development found its centre firmly in the Midlands. No longer the elitist preserve of the white middle classes, the parties had been renamed raves and had started to attract people of all races from every background imaginable.

With Bright's bill in action many of the rave organisers were forced to go legit and put on legal events. The first legal raves were put on by Micky Linus in Coventry and went under the name of Amnesia House, with the first one boasting a line up which included future Junglists Micky Finn and Doc Scott and, for the first time ever, provided a full address for the venue. By this stage the music had started to move away from the Chicago House sounds associated with the early raves. Indeed in a progression which seemed to reflect the anger surrounding the government's rave crackdown, the music took on a new intensity. As more kids got their hands on the samplers needed to produce the music so one of British youth's long held musical obsessions started to surface – the breakbeat.

The breakbeat was originally created by Kool Herc aka Clive Campbell, on the streets of the Bronx. A Jamaican youth who'd arrived in America in 1967, Campbell soon earned the nickname 'Hercules' thanks to his sporting prowess. A few years later he shortened it when a DJing career was thrust upon him. However, he soon discovered that the Reggae records went down like a lead balloon in this neighbourhood. What these kids wanted was some Funk to lose themselves to. Herc soon noticed that the stuff which sent the kids maddest wasn't the actual tracks, but the instrumental breaks of unadulterated waist down, loose booty grooves. Usually as short as eight bars, the breaks represented an explosion of energy which always stopped too soon.

Herc wanted to stretch these sections and soon he developed a style which used identical copies of the record spinning on separate turntables. With his rough and ready protomixing he cut back and forth between records, keeping the breaks going for ages, much to the delight of the block party goers. Kool Herc soon christened this style of extended versioning as the Breakbeat.

From here Herc would buy records purely for their instrumental breaks, cutting and chopping them into his set, soaking the labels off the disc so no one would know where he'd found the break. One of the most famous breaks that he pioneered was the so-called 'Apache' break. A mainstay breakbeat of the Jungle scene, it was originally taken from an Incredible Bongo Band version of the Cliff Richard and The Shadows track 'Apache' and came to epitomise the funky vibe of the breakbeat with its emphasis on the first and third beat.

As the years went on the breakbeat became the backbone of the growth of Hip Hop from the mid 1970s and throughout the 1980s and the soundtrack of the b-boy who developed the wild style break dancing to fit with the music.

A few years later in the early 1980s many of today's Junglists could be found down at London's Covent Garden (among other favourite haunts), lino in hand, spinning on their heads and breaking to the Hip Hop beats booming out of their ghetto blasters. The Breakbeat had become as much the sound of urban Britain as it was the sound of the streets of the Bronx and inevitably these UK b-boys brought their love of Hip Hop to the late 1980s rave.

Still very much in the confines of House this new breed of Rave tune was called Hip House or simply Breakbeat by its supporters. Cuts like Renegade Soundwave's fierce cyber Hip House 'The Phantom' and Unique 3's bleep breaking 'The Theme' started to be played next to Kevin Reece Saunderson's 'Chronic House' while Frankie Bones's 'Bones Breaks' series was also being dropped.

The Breakbeat influence slowly seeped into the rave with Hip House tracks increasingly fading into the mix. Shades of Rhythm's 'Homicide' and

Genaside II's 'Death of the Kamikazee' lighting a new flame in the Rave boiler room.

Forgoing the straight 4/4 beat of House, people increasingly started to rifle through their Hip Hop collections for old breaks to sample, placing them against abrasive Techno refrains which were in turn influenced by the influx of Belgian Nu-beat (a precursor to today's Gabba scene). So called 'hoover' tunes like Joey Beltram's 'Mentasm' became moulded with Hip House to create a frenzied attack of sub bass and searing melody. Meanwhile, the rhythms seemed to get faster by the week. Partially thanks to the productions themselves but also through the DJs forcing open their Technics 1210 turntables and adjusting the variable resistor which governed pitch control. As a result DJs were able to increase the speed of the records to a feverish extreme. The side effect of voices being pitched to helium highs only worked as a tool for increased euphoria among the ravers.

As the beats sped up so too did the lifestyle. Gone was the false positivity of early Acid House parties, instead ravers took the militant route. They were on a mission to rave, twenty-four/seven, all day every day, party people who were living their lives on the edge. People would boast about the amount of Es they'd dropped, in a way reminiscent of the fifteen pints a night lager boys. Living on the absolute edge of reality the ravers were all or nothing a hundred per cent Hardcore. The music reflected this extremity as beats and noises became ever more manic. This was Hardcore, the sound of urban Britain defiant in the face of government opposition, laughing at the media-inspired public outrage, chasing the beat to oblivion and beyond.

The main stomping ground for Hardcore was Midlands-based with clubs like Coventry's Eclipse and Kinetix in Stoke-on-Trent (where famously Goldie is purported to have dropped his first E) creating a vibe which separated the region from the rest of the country. The region buzzed with the sound of Hardcore, attracting DJs from the south like Micky Finn, Jumping Jack Frost, Fabio and Grooverider to an area where Doc Scott and DJ SS were shaping sounds. Meanwhile, as the Midlands rocked to the breaks of Hardcore much of the rest of the country was still caught up in the House scene.

Manchester's A Guy Called Gerald, an artist always noted for his ability to remain on the cutting edge through both his early involvement with 808 State (he co-wrote their 'Pacific State' hit) and his own chart storming Acid anthem 'Voodoo Ray', describes how this faster breakbeat style took him by surprise:

I was booked to do a live PA at this rave in the Midlands. I think it was Grooverider who was playing before me. Anyway he was playing these really fast breakbeats and the kids were just going mad. I hadn't seen anything so manic before, I was totally mesmerised. Suddenly I thought, 'shit these beats are all at least 160 bpm and all my stuff is much slower'. I'd basically planned to play a House set, stuff which had been going down really well everywhere else but I just knew it would be a disaster here. Anyway I had these breaks already looped in the sampler so I just sped them up to the right speed and increased the tempo on the backing tracks. And I played other stuff live. It was totally spontaneous, I just didn't know what was going to happen next. But it went down really well.

Meanwhile a quick trip down the M1 found London's underground rocking to its own tune. Employing many of the same moves as Hardcore, the London sound had become imbued with a much stronger black identity. Events like Rage at Heaven attracted a growing audience of black kids to hear Fabio and Grooverider play while the multiracial atmosphere of London's East End was infamous for its thriving warehouse party scene which buzzed every weekend to the adrenaline rush of this new breed of rough breakbeat.

Sometimes described as the first lady of Jungle, DJ Rap found her inspiration in the pill-popping hedonism of the East End scene. 'I'd be off my nut all of the time,' she confesses. 'I can hardly remember those times, they're such a blur. But I do remember seeing this DJ one night and thinking, "Fuck, I'd love to have a go at playing records." Actually the first thing I thought was "He's a bit of alright" but then I noticed how he was like controlling the crowd and that just blew me away.' Rap actually went on to be the first woman to play the main stage of Roast at London's Astoria on Charing Cross Road. The East End scene proved to be a similar inspiration for DJs and punters alike as the quest for that unending weekend buzz went on. A quest which brought people to Rage.

The inspiration for many of today's Drum 'n' Bass players, Fabio and Grooverider's sets at Rage are legendary. Originally housed in Heaven's upstairs bar the duo soon took over the main room, drawing people from all over the country to catch one of their breathtaking sets. Among these was Goldie who discovered the rave scene through Rage. Having lived in America for a while where he had made a name for himself as a graffiti bomber whilst also selling jewellery (gold teeth a speciality), he returned to the UK to find himself right in the middle of the scene. He soon became a fan of Fabio and Grooverider, hanging around the decks each week, hanging on every track they played.

Rage had a very rare energy for an inner city club. A sweatbox where people seemed to lose all sense of time and space, something special was happening in the walls of this club and the regulars knew it. Even though no one had yet been able to pinpoint it.

Kemistry and Storm were among the regulars at Rage, even taking Goldie along for his first session. 'The first time we went to Rage we queued for three and a half hours to get in and we didn't give a damn,' laughs Storm. 'We just wanted to get into the club so much. When we finally got in we only had about an hour and a half left but it didn't matter because we knew this was something totally different. A really cutting edge thing. It was like we all felt the music was special even then. It had never been heard before.'

Fabio and Grooverider experimented with the decks, pitch shifting plates to plus 8, distorting breaks to a manic level, constantly emphasising the influence of black music in the Rage equation. A similar story was being told across the capital at raves like Freedom, Perception, Telepathy and the Dungeons where the rough breaks attracted a 'melange of Komodo-clad Raggas and bug-eyed b-boys'.

The new Hardcore sound of London became a fresh haunt for the fall-out from the Reggae revival of 1990 which had been typified by Soul II Soul's fusion of the Reggae aesthetic and Hip Hop science. Where Soul II Soul had effectively brought about a culmination of the British slow Hip Hop era, the London Hardcore scene witnessed a coming together of the so-called Funki Dreds and the Ravers.

Crews like Shut Up and Dance added Ragga sampling to the equation and bass lines had started to echo the deep resonance of the dub sound.

Shut Up and Dance may have dropped '5, 6, 7, 8' as far back as 1989 but its adoption as a Rave anthem had been a total surprise to them, written as it was for London's Reggae soundsystems. This East London duo's influence was only now coming through and as London's raves became increasingly multiracial the number of Ragga Hardcore crossovers began to increase.

By 1992 SL2 had released 'On a Ragga Tip' which went on to sell in excess of 200,000 copies. Their follow up track 'Way in My Brain', which extensively borrowed from the European Techno influence Reggae sound of Sleng Teng, did similarly well and by the time Shut Up and Dance's label dropped 'Spliffhead' by the Ragga Twins, this sound had provided a multi-tude of pointers towards the possible future of Hardcore: the Jungle sound.

Just as the authorities had taken note of the numbers being lured by rave, so too did the record industry. Having already gone through the Acid House scene signing people up on unrealistic terms, the labels brought many careers to an abrupt end. Labels wanted their signings to come up with hit records, while the artists wanted to stay true to the underground House ethic and experiment.

Similarly artists wouldn't play the star game, ignoring record label requests to have their photos on record sleeves or even entertain the press. The industry had failed to grasp the fact that this was a DJ-led thing, where anonymity was far more important than stardom. It was very much a hang on from the Ecstasy induced vibe that no one was more important than the scene. Inevitably the major industry started to drop these problem acts as quickly as they signed them.

Gerald Simpson (aka A Guy Called Gerald) was one artist who became dogged by record label hassles. Signed to CBS on the strength of 'Voodoo Ray', the label found it hard to accept that he was someone with a passion for sound experimentation; instead they tried to force Gerald into the narrow confines of the hit single market. 'Up until then the industry saw all dance music in the same terms as disco,' explains Gerald. 'Basically a dis-posable product aimed at a black audience. They thought like it was a minority form of music so it had to be pushed in that way. They just couldn't understand what it was we were doing.'

The record industry had a similar lack of understanding when it came to Hardcore. However, by this time a number of smaller labels had learned the industry well enough to compete. Independent labels with their hearts still sold on the rave scene started to promote the Hardcore sound which in turn started to produce records which dented the national charts.

Then The Prodigy dropped 'Charlie'. A Breakbeat anthem based around a cartoon cat from a 1970s public information film, the record stormed the charts, going straight into the top ten. A ground breaking record in that it opened the eyes of a lot of producers to the possibilities offered by cutting up and rearranging the breakbeats rather than simply looping them in an adoption of Hip Hop's beats. (It wasn't the first, but it was certainly the best known!) 'Charlie's success showed the first signs of this music's marketability.

For many it presented an easy way of making a fast buck and suddenly a flurry of Rave tunes aimed specifically at the Top of the Pops market arrived. So-called Toytown Rave, the tunes became typified by 'Rhubarb and Custerd', 'Sesame's Treat' and 'Trip to Trumpton'. For many it marked the end of the rave. Already the events had degenerated into places where young kids wore white gloves, snorted Vick's nasal inhalers and wore ski masks, all in an attempt to prolong the buzz of the drugs which themselves were rarely what they were being sold as. Many pills confiscated were found to be cut with chemicals ranging from low quality amphetamine through to completely harmless food products like flour, although the media suggested that such things as fish tank cleaner and rat poison had been found in samples they had procured. The truth is, however, that Ecstasy on sale rarely contained more than the smallest trace of MDMA.

People were being ripped off continually as the dealers raked in a fortune from the ravers. However, it wasn't only the unscrupulous dealings of the drug pushers who were intent on making a fast buck from the illegal trade of raving. Many bogus promoters would sell tickets for imaginary events, preying on people's nostalgia and love for the days of illegal raving. Full colour flyers boasting all-star line ups would be printed and tickets were sold at a cost of £25 and over through the usual outlets (dance record shops, etc.). The numbers to call could only be obtained from the ticket itself and since it had long been the practice to give only mobile numbers nothing would be suspected to be amiss until the night of the rave when the number never got connected.

Worse still were the practices of the legal promoters who would regularly print names on their flyers for DJs who weren't actually booked. Only when you'd arrived at the event did you discover that the line up consisted of unknowns who invariably couldn't mix. Grooverider particularly became a target for this trick. Knowing his name would guarantee ticket sales, it would constantly be printed on tickets for raves in the Midlands. In the event his non-appearance would be put down to a no-show rather than the promoter's devious greed, and Grooverider soon gained a bad reputation.

By 1992 the rave had become a parody of itself, the Toytown ravers representing the final selling out of the scene. Those people who still professed to 'know the score' were left with no other option but to react, rebel and go underground once more.

It was the long winter after a time when anything had seemed possible. Economically the entire nation was experiencing a soul destroying slump which had made the affluent 1980s seem very far off indeed. Politically, the nations ravers had witnessed a government hell bent on outlawing their chosen lifestyle. Within the raves, unscrupulous dealers were cutting the Ecstasy with any old rubbish, and the most accessible type of pill was the ultra heavy 'Snowball'. Not MDMA but an enormous quantity of MDA. A much stronger and longer lasting drug, it had the opposite effect to MDMAs up-all-night buzz. Instead it turned people into zombies. People would lie around 'monged out' as the so-called 'smacky' effects of the drug took their toll. The rave it would seem was up to its eyes in Snowballs and almost certainly on its last legs.

The mood of the whole country was sombre and as if once more reflecting both social and subcultural conditions, the music became darkly aggressive, rhythmically frantic, with treble boosted breakneck beats running at between 150 and 160 bpms and mixed with a half time subsonic b-line; the four to the floor kick drum conspicuous by its absence.

Like the social conditions which were shaping it, the music was called 'Dark'. A disconcerting marriage of Rave's 'on a mission' hedonism and Dancehall's 'trust nobody' suss, this sound was eventually to become known as Jungle. A style which placed the metallic edge of Hardcore next to the entire lexicon of black music, from Ragga to House, Sleng Teng to Techno.

RECOMMENDED LISTENING

'We Are E' – Lennie De Ice (De Underground)

'Mr Kirk's Nightmare' – 4 Hero (Reinforced)

'The Theme' – Unique 3 (Warp)

'On A Ragga Tip' – SL2 (XL)

'Way in My Brain' – SL2 (XL)

'5, 6 7, 8' – Shut Up and Dance (SUAD)

'Illegal Gunshot' – The Ragga Twins (SUAD)

'Mentasm' – Second Phase (R&S)

'Insomniac' – DJPC (Hype)

'Dancin' People' – Q Bass (Suburban Base)

'Further Out' – Sonz of a Loop da Loop Era (Suburban Base)

'Waremouse' – 2 Bad Mice (Moving Shadow)

'Space Cakes' – Kaotic Chemistry (Moving Shadow)

'Music Takes You' – Blame (Moving Shadow)

3: VALLEY OF THE SHADOWS

THE MEDIA BLACKOUT AND THE RISE OF DARK

With the onset of Toytown Rave the media finally found justification for its relative lack of coverage of the Hardcore phenomenon. Raves were now the stomping ground for drug dealing gangs, white gloved kids and unscrupulous promoters. The ravers themselves had become known as 'cheesy quavers', the total antithesis to the cool conscious Progressive House scene which was coming to dominate the country's clubs.

Immediately championed by the dance publications like *Mixmag*, the Progressive House scene adopted a similar elitist ethos as the Balearic and Acid House days, with many of the faces of 1988 cropping up once again. For publications like *Mixmag* the raves had become too moody, arenas where the threat of violence seemed to hang in the air, replacing the previous atmosphere of togetherness.

The Progressive House development offered the perfect chance to resurrect feelings of old, feelings which were typified by 1987's legendary Shoom club. This nostalgic reaction led to a rediscovery of the roots of House. And, in an ironic twist of fate, the very artists that the Breakbeat DJs paid most respect to, took their place as champions of the media. Old Chicago producers were once again looked to for inspiration while Detroit's Techno old skool was held aloft. The dance scene increasingly looked abroad for the music, the artists and the story. The grass, it would seem, was certainly greener on the other side of the Atlantic.

Meanwhile the weekly music press, long suspicious of Rave's promotion of artists' anonymity adopted the burgeoning Ambient Techno scene and the movement towards live dance bands. Acts like Orbital, The Orb and Transglobal Underground easily assimilated into the star system requirements of both *NME* and *Melody Maker*, were presented as 'the dance bands it's OK to like'. Events like Club Dog and Whirl-y-Gig, with their largely middle class anti-establishment ethos, dominated while journalists continued to suggest that Hardcore was simply music for stupid people. Indeed in a move echoed by the Drum 'n' Bass scene a few years later, Ambient was increasingly promoted as 'intelligent' techno.

While these media obsessions may have been justified by the endless list of classic records produced, the emphasis had moved so far away from the Hardcore Breakbeat movement that had come to represent the true underground sound of the UK. What was effectively a media blackout merely created the space for the Breakbeat producers to develop in their own way; without the constant glare of the media to stifle creativity.

With the gradual closure of raves, Hardcore and Breakbeat clubs and the media blackout, avenues for exposure rapidly closed down. The producers retreated to their studios to take the sound through a series of contortions, morphing it into the psychotic depth charges known as 'Dark'.

DARK

Dark came with the feeling of breakdown in society. It was winter, clubs were closing, the country was in decline. As an artist I had to reflect it.

Goldie

Very much a reaction against the dodgy raves, the pop tendencies of Toytown and the dominance of Happy Hardcore within the remaining rave scene, Dark also presented a reflection of the times. It was 1993 and the nation was gripped by the worst economic slump in years. The cost of living was soaring, unemployment prevailed and houses were being repossessed after the 'never had it so good' bubble of the 1980s had finally burst.

The people who were being hit the hardest were those already living on the breadline. Twelve years previously the inner city housing estates had united against the authorities in a series of nationwide riots. In 1993 however the sense of unity in the face of authority became increasingly represented by the proliferation of black marketeering. An underclass had fully evolved where mass unemployment (invariably spanning people's entire adult life) hit families hard. Urban youth had next to no chance of gaining meaningful work and the gradual introduction of student loans started to shut down the possibilities of escape through the education system. The only possibilities the system seemed to offer were the Youth Training Schemes, which paid little more than pocket money for a full week's work and provided little real training.

As a result an alternative black market culture of scamming arose. Drug dealing, thieving and dole fiddling became commonplace. People living in the inner cities of Britain were increasingly forced to live this underclass lifestyle as the very fabric of society crumbled.

An attitude which has been central to the Junglist's 'trust nobody' identity grew out of this subterranean lifestyle. In these housing estates a different set of principles was starting to become commonplace, principles which held up the sense of disenfranchisement which abounded. From Goldie's youth in the urban wastelands of the Midlands to Jumping Jack Frost's upbringing among London's tower blocks, most of Jungle's originators grew up in these surroundings subsequently imbibing Jungle with the same set of underclass values.

Dark, or Darkcore as it was also called, found Rave at its most sombre. A sound which was typified by Goldie's 'Terminator'. A wash of minor chords and brooding sonics it presented a horror show of epic proportions, haunted throughout by a repeated phrase lifted from Japan's 'Ghosts'. A nightmare vision of a cyborg future, possessed by the spirit of human frailty. 'The ghosts of my life' refrain echoed over a Breakbeat which twisted and span in all directions, cutting the ether with a surgeon's precision. Belting out of a club soundsystem 'Terminator' seemed to get deep inside your cranium, pushing and pulling your mind in untold directions.

A truly groundbreaking track, 'Terminator' was the first time that the timestretching technique had been used on the breaks; an effect which allows you to alter tempo without changing the pitch. Subsequently 'Terminator' was able to speed up without it ever feeling like the track was playing any faster. The result: a phenomenal sense of unadulterated exhilaration.

Of course the signs that this kind of dark intensity would emerge had been around for a long time prior to 'Terminator'. In 1991 4 Hero released an astonishing track named 'Mr Kirk's Nightmare'. A fast and hard Breakbeat monster it took the listener through the darkest fears of Ecstasy paranoia. Playing on the tabloid hysteria about Ecstasy related deaths the Reinforced crew took every parent's nightmare and turned it into a twisted scenario of comic tragedy. 'I'm sorry Mr Kirk you better come down to the station house. Your son is dead. Dead? How? He died of an overdose.'

It was a track which actually nearly destroyed DJ Rap's career. During one particular rave the tune seemed almost prophetic. Someone actually died just as Rap, ignorant of the unfolding tragedy, dropped the tune! As if still shocked by the experience, she explains:

I played at this rave called Telepathy and someone got stabbed. There was this record around at the time called 'Mr Kirk's Nightmare'. Guess who played it just as the guy got stabbed? I didn't realise it had happened but the result was that I lost every booking I'd ever worked for. When the police came to my house they said 'So you're the DJ everyone hates'. I had no idea this guy had been stabbed but people didn't believe me.

Despite its association with a specific tragedy, 'Mr Kirk's Nightmare' captured a mood of defiance among the ravers, encapsulating a feeling that was literally becoming a case of do or die. When the reality came to stare people in the face, however, the tune took on a fresh intensity. There was almost a nihilistic energy among the ravers, an energy which pushed people to their limits. The sonic equivalent of sky surfing, bungee jumping or Russian roulette, this feeling surfaced again on tracks like Lennie de Ice's apocalyptic 'We Are E'.

Meanwhile with the stunning Breakbeat manipulation on 'Mass Confusion', 2 Bad Mice took the theme through deeper contortions, cutting up breaks which slid in and out of perspective, chasing each other in a breakneck race to oblivion, a satanic voice repeatedly saying 'diffusion' over the beats.

If there was a defining moment for Hardcore's entry into the Dark period, however, it must surely have arrived with Doc Scott's astounding 'Here Comes the Drumz'. Released in mid 1992 it took the Breakbeat

Ambience deep into a state of manic psychosis. Metallic, militaristic drums stepped an insistent path through cyber-tech terrorscapes. Where Goldie's 'Terminator' had danced with bleak visions of the future, 'Drumz' went straight into battle with them.

This was a time when video libraries offered endless possibilities for sampling. Discordant strings and haunting refrains would be lifted from horror films, dislocated ambience appropriated from science fiction movies. Occasionally phrases were lifted whole and placed in a track for added poignance, creating a filmesque chemical comedown. Never was this more powerful than on Origin Unknown's 'Valley of the Shadows'. By combining rolling and thundering breaks with sub bass intensity, Essex boys Ant Miles and Andy C created a Dantesque vision of hell in the urbanscape. The addition of a girl in the grip of paralytic fear mumbling the phrase 'I felt that I was in a long dark tunnel' turned it into a disturbing piece of Breakbeat *noir* that Coppola would have been proud of.

Inevitably the Horrorcore visions of Dark were taken too far by some. Believing this to be a satanistic movement the scene started to attract its fair share of devil worshipping nutters. Dark quickly gained a reputation as Rave's version of Death Metal with people talking of hidden messages in the tracks. 'All these kids have turned it into a joke. They think Dark is about devil worship,' complained Goldie in an interview with *Vibe* in early 1994.

In reality the Dark sound had less to do with worshipping at the altar of Beelzebub and more to do with the developments in technology which somehow enhanced the creative mood of the times. This may have been the era when the art of timestretching was first explored but the proliferation of horror samples came from people actually discovering what they could do by actually altering the pitch down on the sampler keyboard.

Pete Parsons was in-house engineer for Dee Jay Recordings and Lucky Spin throughout this period. As a result he worked on a multitude of classic tracks including DJ Crystal's seminal 'Warpdrive' where both he and the DJ developed a strong working relationship. The same was true of his partnership with DJ Rap on the duo's album *Intelligent*. However, at a time when many of the people creating tracks were DJs with a couple of ideas and an armful of records to sample, the engineers were rapidly becoming the unsung heroes of the scene, slaving over a hot mixing desk, tweaking the finer requirements and sifting through the mathematics of sampling while the DJ sat in the background, smoking copious quantities of ganja and occasionally nodding his head when things were sounding good. For the actual knob pushers like Parsons the final insult would come when the record would come out with the DJ's name emblazoned across the label, while the engineer's moniker was effectively the almost hidden small print.

However, when DJs did venture to the keyboard they would frequently be amazed by the sounds they were playing. Sounds which Parsons et al. were rarely excited by. Parsons, carefully not naming names, reminisces:

You'd get these people playing around on the keyboard. There would be a bit of a dialogue sampled across the whole keyboard and people would play things really low down and think that it was fucking amazing, like the best thing they'd ever heard. For the engineers it was quite normal really, but somehow these deep voices fitted into the music which we were making deliberately horrible, just to keep people out.

As the Dark sound gained popularity it quickly began to take on comic proportions. The sounds got bleaker, the vocal samples became more obvious, less and less the product of creative minds at work, but the sound of Dark's sheep following the leaders.

However, as has been the case throughout the history of Jungle, the scene's main movers had already moved on to different pastures, disregarding Dark as a passing phase and taking its spiritual essence fast forward to the future.

A.W.O.L.

In March 1992 The Paradise Club in Islington, London, opened its doors to the A.W.O.L. crew. A weekly event dedicated to Breakbeat science, A.W.O.L. very quickly became the meeting place for ex-ravers still dedicated to the post-Hardcore vibe.

With the closure of Rage at Heaven, The Paradise became the scene's epicentre. A club where the regulars were checked out and duly acknowledged and the newcomers treated with suspicion until they'd proven themselves to the established regulars. A venue which boasted an oppressive gloom, a vision-impairing thick fog of ganja continuously hanging in the air. The A.W.O.L. soundsystem belted out a relentless stream of Darkcore and Breakbeat Techno interspersed with MC shout outs and splashes of Ragga toasting.

The club presented the face of urban militancy. A tougher-than-you street attitude which was typified by the very phrase that A.W.O.L. stood for – A Way Of Life. For the regulars this music went far beyond merely love of the sound, turning into an obsessional, all-encompassing lifestyle. This was a twenty-four/seven existence where the true Hardcore stuck together and the weekenders just didn't figure.

Pulling some of the scene's biggest names of the time, A.W.O.L. featured resident DJs Randall, Micky Finn, Darren Jay, Kenny Ken and Dr S. Gachet, all pushing the soundsystem to its limits and working the crowd like a V8 engine.

Where the club originally had a sense of euphoria surrounding it, the gradual introduction of Dark, until it finally took over after three months, changed the atmosphere totally. A.W.O.L. had become unlike any of the E'd-up raves of old. Increasingly the vibe was strictly heads down, feel the beat and move. Whereas previously a loss of control was celebrated, here total control was paramount. Inevitably outsiders who came down for the first time found the vibe too heavy, the people too shifty. But A.W.O.L. had a different club language, one which suited this new sound and took more than just one visit to become fully conversant.

The Paradise was also different from the old rave due to the closeness of both the DJ and the crowd. At A.W.O.L. they were literally on top of each other. As a result the DJ was forced to read the vibe of the crowd and listen to their reactions. Taking many of the styles of the Reggae soundsystem clashes the audience would let their feelings be known in no uncertain terms. Air horns rang out and shouts of 'rewind' were increasingly heard. Soon the MCs would pick up on the demands and join the call. 'Rewind, rewind operator', shouted the crowd. The DJ was forced to spin the disc backwards as the MC chatted, holding the intro back to build up the suspense until the crowd was at fever pitch and then bringing the beats back in with a rush of pure adrenaline. A magical experience which created a unique atmosphere. As Randall explained at the time:

A.W.O.L. is the club with the best vibe. When you play there, the atmosphere is so close and the crowd is so near you that it's like home, there is a really homely effect. Shouting for rewinds started in Paradise, because the crowd was going so crazy there was just no other option. That was when the Jungle started coming on strong, when Paradise was stinging and the system was so loud it was too much. I was there the other week at seven o'clock in the morning and the place was unreal – it was rammed!

An overcrowded sweatbox which provided the ultimate Jungle rush, A.W.O.L. at The Paradise was *the* club which gave the scene its first sense of a real identity. It truly became the home of the Junglists. Inevitably the reign of the club saw the rise in popularity in the use of the term 'Jungle' and in many ways the scene was finally fully formed as faces which had been seen both at Rage and London's East End warehouse parties came together to shape the future.

GANGSTA RAVE

As the Jungle scene has solidified, it's taken on a criminal-minded identity – call it Gangsta Rave. It reflects a desperate reality . . . the soundtrack of Britain's burgeoning underclass, black and white kids alike who live in the same tower blocks and estates and share the same hatred of the police and love of the chronic.

Simon Reynolds, Vibe

The unified vibe of A.W.O.L. was shortlived as different groups soon jostled to take control within the scene. The increased proliferation of Ragga samples and the adoption of the Reggae soundclash vibe had started to attract the criminal Yardie element to the club. Punters would talk of being mugged in the toilets, while on the dancefloor people talked of the distinctive smell of crack which started to permeate the air. Strongly denied at the time by those punters desperate to cling to the old A.W.O.L. vibe, for many others the club had changed. Many of the early A.W.O.L. faces realised that the time had come to move on as once again the close family atmosphere had been ruptured. 'It was like you'd be taking your life into your own hands when you went to the toilet,' says Joe, one ex-punter who watched the vibe change. 'It just got really heavy, I mean I was used to the heavy vibes of some of the things in the East End but this was like nothing I'd ever seen. I stopped going when one night this geezer just comes straight up to me and smacks me in the mouth almost as soon as I'd arrived.'

Marc Royal, a regular at A.W.O.L. from the outset, talks of a similar increase in heavy vibes, arguing that this was down to the introduction of crack which was brought into the club as Dark took a greater hold, the sound itself fitting perfectly with the crack vibe. With anger still audible in his voice, he argues:

I watched the Dark sound bring crack into the rave and that's a fact which certain people are running away from. Dark brought crack into the raves, it's then when things went moody. I went to The Paradise Club for the first twenty odd weeks and until then there was no trouble. Now you could ask whether music has that much effect on people; well yes evidently it does. Hip Hop gun culture has brought a whole new generation of b-boys who have bought into the major label perspective of what Hip Hop is about and it's created a violent generation of b-boys. The same thing has happened over here with the rave scene. Whether that has got something to do with the whole idea of people waking up at the end of this great dream of the 'Second Summer of Love' in 1989 and going, 'Hang on a minute, the country is actually fucked', or whether it was simply the music; well the music obviously helps it along.

Indeed the Dark sound was much heavier than the old Happy Hardcore sound of the Rave days and it could be said that this new Horrorcore music simply attracted a crack head mentality in the same way that Psychedelic music of the 1970s attracted people into acid. Whether or not the music itself has the power to influence people's drug use is debatable as both the music and the associated lifestyle are too inextricably linked to consider separately. However, for a number of the people involved in the scene, even the slightest association between Dark and crack is both ridiculous and dangerous. Dego McFarlane of Reinforced Records, one of the prime exponents of Dark, feels that this brings an immediate assumption that the people behind the music are both advocators and users of crack: 'You know, who ever says that wants to shut the fuck up,' shouts Dego, amazed that Dark and crack could be considered to walk hand in hand. 'The first Dark records that were made were not made by crack heads and neither are they now. I ain't on crack and I don't think Ed Rush is on crack and I don't think Dillinger is either. In fact, what I see these days is like maybe people smoking weed or whatever. You don't need to be on nothing to get the Dark sound. The Dark sound is a result of the technology creating it.'

The reality was that crack had become a minor feature of a Jungle scene which had taken on many of the same value as the Gangsta rappers of America. In early 1993 DJ Ron, noted for his heavy leanings towards the Ragga-Jungle vibe, dropped 'Crackman on the Line'. A sinister brew of bad vibes and Jump Up energy, while not condoning crack use, the track acknowledged that crack had found a home with a few individuals in the Jungle scene.

A much heavier scene started to emerge where people talked of knife point muggings at Jungle raves. As seen at A.W.O.L., you were as likely to get mugged in the toilets as you were to get offered dodgy gear on the dancefloor. To any outsider the scene seemed to boast an extremely aggressive underworld presence and unsurprisingly, Junglists started to gain a wider reputation for the scene's association with crack cocaine. A fact which was instantly jumped upon by the sensationalist media who used it as a further reason to disregard the fertile creativity of Breakbeat's producers and DJs. In a feature about Wolverhampton Jungle club Quest and the nascent Ragga-Jungle scene, *Mixmag*'s Jane Headon described with horror her realisation that crack was present in Jungle clubs:

. . . there are reports of Jungle clubs that are much rougher. Where people get attacked and where crack is openly used. This happened to me at a Jungle night: Two fifteen-year-olds spotted my friend's hash pipe and asked if they could use it. A moment later there was an unpleasant sweetish smell. 'What are you smoking?' he asked. 'Snood,' they replied, giggling inanely. 'Snood?' 'Yeah, snood, you know, snood, crack. You want some?'

The report brought about instant rebuttals, with Dark's vanguard denying emphatically that crack was associated with the scene. The break-beat front line had already faced years of persecution through the media

thanks to the Ecstasy frenzy. The last thing that this economically flourish-
ing and creatively unparalleled movement needed now was a media con-
centration on crack in the Jungle.

In reality, however, at the same time as crack cocaine had surfaced
among the Junglists, so too had it raised its ugly head throughout clubland;
its sickly sweet aroma filling the air of many of the UK's inner city House
clubs. 'Music has always been associated with drugs, always,' argues DJ
Storm in defence of Jungle. 'But it was wrong to associate crack with us.
Sure we were into E for a while but the crack scene was something which
just attached itself to Drum 'n' Bass. Mostly people were just into smoking
weed at that point.' It's a point backed up by Dego McFarlane who takes it
even further by suggesting that the pinning of crack use on the Jungle scene
smacked of the scapegoat tactics of racism:

Drugs are everywhere in every club but they [the media] used us as a
scapegoat for crack. The Hip Hop scene was used as a scapegoat for
censorship while Heavy Metal bands were saying the same kind of shit and
no one was doing nothing. In the same way Drum 'n' Bass was getting a rep
for crack and that kind of shit was going on at the House clubs where people
were off their faces. That shit always happens. Someone's always making
me the scapegoat and they don't want to look in the other places.

Jungle's 'bad boy' image started to prevail and the repercussions were
felt throughout the scene as clubs closed their doors to these so-called
'troublemakers and crack heads'. Junglists who were interested in the scene
for the music were having a rough time. Clubs would turn away anyone
dressed in styles associated with Ragga. Furthermore, some West End clubs
had developed door policies which verged on apartheid in their exclusion of
'undesirables'. Although the club management or promoters would never
admit an involvement in such practices, the rave scene had long known that
club security people were a law unto themselves. As such they laid down
the law and the black Junglists were increasingly being turned away from
the raves. 'I've been to certain raves – gone to a rave and not gone to rob
anybody or whatever – but because I dress a certain way I've been turned
away,' explained James of Third Party and the Kemet Crew who was among

the many affected. He continued:

One particular time one of our tunes was playing when I was standing in the queue! That must have been a sign for me. Me and my partner at the time said: 'Boy, this can't be real, man. We make the music, and the people are raving to our music and we're being turned away from the clubs.' We said, well, we'll Jungle it. We'll Jungle it all up. If they're saying that we can't get in there because we look a certain way or we're a certain colour, then we'll Jungle it and create our own thing.

In Chris Campion's overview of the Jungle scene in USA's *URB Magazine* he draws from the normally candid subjects a series of brutally honest quotes. If the Junglists interviewed were to be believed, the greater club scene had developed an unhealthy taste for racial exclusion largely due to the reputation of a few outsiders who had attached themselves to Jungle. In the same interview, Mark X outlines the irony of this racism. Jungle itself was not simply a black rudeboy thing as it was increasingly portrayed, but the product of a multicultural Britain. 'It's the name that causes the divisions, that causes the upset. Now we know it's got its white element, it's got its black element. You got UK Apache come in with the Indian style of things. It's for all who would listen to it, who would love it.'

There was however another side to the exclusion of Junglists from the raves. Clubbers had become extremely vocal in their disdain for Jungle and its dark vibes. Wherever the Junglists were, the atmosphere of the rave apparently changed. Into the heartland of the chemically induced bonhomie of Ecstasy's smiley children came Jungle's moodiness. Each month the letters columns of *Generator* and *Mixmag* would feature extended rants about how the music was too dark for the Happy Hardcore crews and how the Junglists were killing the vibe. Some clubs had even taken to displaying signs declaring the venue a 'No Breakbeat Zone' in order both to dissuade Junglists from entering and to confirm their allegiance to the House crowd.

In his *i-D* feature 'Jungle! Jungle! The last Dance Underground', cultural theorist Kodwo Eshun suggested that Jungle's presence had come to represent the destruction of Rave's naive Utopian ideals: 'All too often, the dislike of Jungle translates into a fear of the Alien Ruffneck, of the Rudeboy from the council estate who's supposedly spoilt the peace-and-love vibe and the dream of trans-tribal unity. Jungle, so this racist myth goes, is what killed Smiley, turned every raver's little Woodstock into an Altamont with bassbins.'

Jungle was (and is), as Mark X has suggested, very much a multi-racial thing, a movement which has always celebrated its sense of multi-racial Britishness via its myriad influences. Yet Jungle continued to draw many of Rave's deep seated prejudices to the surface as talk abounded of violence, crack and muggings which came to be the stereotypical definition of the Junglists amid the House scene. Furthermore the rumours persisted that it was simply asking for trouble if you were a white male in a Jungle rave. Despite the fact that a great many of the DJs, producers and indeed punters were white.

In 1994 Paul Chambers, who formed Ibiza Records, the label respons-ible for first using the 'Jungle Tekno' tag for compilation albums, suggested to *The Face* that this fear was a mainly male orientated thing, asking: 'Why are the majority of girls at Jungle raves white? They're not scared. It's the blokes that are scared.' The truth of this white male fear may have had many sociological and psychological connotations. However, the simple fact remained that Jungle presented a threat to the House hegemony and as a result it was slowly becoming segregated from the rest of the House scene as increasingly Breakbeat DJs weren't being booked and the Jungle fra-ternity was being turned away from club doors.

With this kind of exclusion being mirrored by the media, the scene turned further inwards towards developing its own exclusivity where only the true Hardcore Junglists were accepted and the media were most defi-nitely unwelcome.

The hundred per cent Jungle rave started to emerge in late 1993, dis-playing just how popular the Jungle phenomenon had become. Much to the chagrin of many of the scene's originators, however, leading this growth in popularity were the Ragga-Junglists.

RECOMMENDED LISTENING

'Terminator' – Metalheads (Reinforced)

'Here Comes The Drumz' – Doc Scott (Reinforced)

'Valley of the Shadows' – Origin Unknown (Ram)

'Bludclot Artattack' – Ed Rush (white)

'Lord of the Null Lines' – Hyper on Experience (white)

'Helicopter Tune' – Deep Blue (Moving Shadow)

'Warpdrive' – DJ Crystal (Lucky Spin)

'The Pulse' – DJSS (Formation Records)

'Eye Memory' – Nebula II (Reinforced)

'Last Action Hero' – Doc Scott (Reinforced)

4: ARMED AND DANGEROUS

RAGGA-JUNGLE TAKES CONTROL

Wicked, wicked Junglist massive. Big up the original Junglist massive. The original dancestyle Junglist . . . incredible.

'Incredible' M Beat featuring General Levy

Ragga was the sound of defiance. A solidification of cultural unity in the face of the dominant white British culture. The music presented a barrage of militant Reggae beats with sound effects mutated from the dub systems. The lyrics, which seemed indecipherable to anyone not ensconced in the culture, were a redeployment of the patois language of resistance. It was free-flowing street slang which used overtly sexual phrasing coupled with direct in-your-face posturing. In the dancehalls of Britain's black communities Ragga was the main sound. So popular was it that specialist shops reported import record sales which challenged even the national top twenty with its ability to sell.

Ragga's roots are placed firmly in the Reggae soundsystem tradition. During the 1970s, instrumental mixes of tracks would be given to the DJ on acetate (dub plate). An extremely up front copy of the forthcoming record release, the acetates would have limited playability. Originally made of a clay compound but now metal based, the quality of the sound would deteriorate with repeated plays. The original acetates may have had as short a life as five plays before the tune would be obliterated by pops and crackles on the surface of the disc.

The acetate would have an enormous kudos value with DJs begging the top studio houses for these up front sounds. To get one meant you'd been acknowledged as an important face on the scene, a potential taste-maker. It's a form of hierarchy which has been taken on board lock, stock and barrel among the Junglists, with producers providing the chosen few with DAT tapes of their latest tunes, which in turn get stamped up as an acetate version.

With the acetate of the instrumental version playing on the sound-system, the Reggae MC would then chat his own lyrics over the tune thus creating an entirely different track. It's a style which has been adopted by every DJ led scene since, creating the spark for new genres to appear, Hip Hop and Ragga being the most notable.

The MCing style was initially given the name 'toasting'. Perhaps the best known of these vocalists was U-Roy whose 1969 recordings with pro-ducer King Tubby have been hugely influential ever since. U-Roy is often referred to as 'The Originator', thanks to his incredibly distinctive style which found an exaggeration of the phonetic structures of words used as rhythmical instruments. Distorting words and rhymes to suit his own needs, U-Roy's combination of rap, scat, chat and singing eventually spawned a generation of imitators. I-Roy, Big Youth and Dennis Alcapone came forward and a whole new style of Reggae emerged – Dancehall style.

Dancehall itself uses an MC style which employs the stylised broken English of patois. This approach was taken further by the significant Jamaican populations in Britain and America, introducing localised street slang into the equation, and the patois of the MCs turned into a style known as Raggamuffin. Perhaps the earliest example can be found on Prince Jammy, aka Wayne Smith's 1985 track 'Under Mi Sleng Teng'. Not only did this track spawn a new musical style known as Sleng Teng, a sound inspired by the Casio bleeps prevalent on Soul Sonic Force's 'Planet Rock' but it also hinted at a new vocal delivery.

'Under Mi Sleng Teng' went on to become one of the most versioned tracks in the history of Reggae. One notable example which was particu-larly influential on the Hardcore scene was SL2's 'Way in My Brain', which lifted the techno buzz of the Sleng Teng bass line in its entirety. Wayne Smith's original managed to dupe the radio authorities into sanctioning air-play for a record which talked about smoking ganja. However, the language used was the Ragga language which the radio jocks simply didn't understand.

Ragga became increasingly prevalent, its terminology adopted as the anti-system language of the street, adapted to suit each new generation of user. In Britain the authorities were totally confounded by a linguistic style with which the youth population, black, white and Asian, of the inner cities was completely conversant. It became a true language of opposition which had crossed over the race barrier and had come to provide the street lexicon of disenfranchised youth.

Throughout 1992 and 1993 the Reggae underground had rocked to the Dancehall vibe of Ragga's ruling MCs – Buju Banton, Topcat and Shabba Ranks. However, the Ragga sound wasn't totally in step with the younger generation of black Britons who, inspired by the success of SL2's 'On a Ragga Tip' and The Ragga Twins's 'Spliffhead', were increasingly being attracted by the clarion call of the rave. In turn Ragga licks were adapted to the sound of Hardcore, subsequently taking an ever more influential position in the Rave soundtrack. By late 1993 Breakbeat Jungle had become so interlinked with Ragga that the two seemed almost synonymous.

It was almost inevitable that the combination of the 160 bpm breaks of Hardcore and the 80 bpm bass lines of Reggae would eventually bring people to the Ragga vocal. The two styles seemed to complement each other completely and, unlike most vocal samples, the Ragga vocal was already pitched at the right tempo. However, the earliest records to filter through containing Ragga vocals were simply cases of straight sampling rather than employing live MCs.

An increasingly dominant studio production tool was the sample CD. A series of commercially produced discs containing a library of sounds, they became an integral part of any studio set up. Ideal for the engineer knocking out tracks in the few hours booked by the DJs to produce their tracks, perfect for the lone boffins cooking up bad Breakbeat alchemy in their bedrooms. The sounds contained would range from the latest bass frequency to more exotic selections like monks chanting or versions of the Koran. Inevitably the Ragga lick became one of the CD production companies' commodities.

As producers explored the studio sample CDs looking for the hook to lift their tune above the others, they would stumble on a series of Ragga rhymes ready to be lifted. With the pressure of studio cost (or the lack of live vocal facilities), the ready made samples were a quick, easy and cheap option. Producers started to exploit these CD samplers fully and a flood of so-called Ragga crossover tracks flooded the market.

Ragga refrains by complete unknowns would subsequently sit next to all of the scene's best known names on Jungle dub plates, but the crowds at the Jungle raves didn't care. It was the Ragga vibe they wanted and this substandard version helped push the euphoria, so the quick-buck engineers and producers continued to push invariably substandard tracks at the scene.

Not all of the Ragga-Jungle tracks to be released were pale versions of the respective elements, however. Among the first tracks to emerge which combined Ragga elements with the rough breaks of Jungle came out on A Guy Called Gerald's Juicebox imprint. Initially a series of 12s but ultimately collected together on the '28 Gun Bad Boy' compilation, this material gained instant respect among the Darkcore crews. It also led the way for a series of classic tracks like Potential Bad Boy's 'Warning-remix' or indeed the startlingly dark 'The Burial' by Leviticus. But it wasn't until the Jungle producers started to use live vocalists that the scene really started to blow up.

Among the best known of the Ragga-Jungle tunes was 'Original Nuttah' by Shy FX and rising Asian Ragga star UK Apache. Essentially a reworked version of Shy FX's 'Gangsta Kid', which featured the vocals of Gunsmoke, it had been released in early 1993 on SOUR's formative DJ Only label. Excited by the huge potential in combining vocals with Jungle, SOUR A&R man Vini Medley had thought of the possibility of putting Apache and Shy together after hearing some of the former's stuff coming out of the Ibiza Records HQ.

By coincidence Apache had apparently been secretly using a 'Gangsta Kid' loop as a backing track for one of his lyrics, so when the idea was suggested for the two to collaborate they both went straight with it. In the event, 'Original Nuttah' was recorded in only one studio take and the end result was put out on dub at the end of 1993. Given to selected DJs like Hype and Ron, they instantly started caning the tune at the raves. The response was amazing, with kids hanging around the DJ box trying to work out who the record was by. Once word had leaked the specialist shops were inundated with orders for the tune. Kool FM rinsed it out, playing it on just about every show subsequently pushing demand higher. Vini Medley even recalls going into shops with a box of white labels only to see people bartering for the records. An auction room atmosphere prevailed with white labels fetching up to £30 a piece. With a glint in his eye, Vini recalls:

It was just totally insane, man. People just wanted the tune so bad. A lot of the demand came from that year's [Notting Hill] Carnival, it was being played constantly; people shouting for rewinds all of the time. The Jungle soundclashes helped as well. In fact Kenny Ken won one of these soundclashes with 'Original Nuttah'. Shy had recorded a new version for him that went 'You never know the article, genuine in the Jungle, you never know Kenny Ken he rule the Jungle'. They went fucking insane when they heard it and he got ten rewinds on it. Actually he beat Rap who got seven rewinds with the same tune. But she hadn't got the special version! Actually every DJ played 'Nuttah' that night!

By the time 'Original Nuttah' was released in August 1994 it was one of the most sought after records on the scene and as a result it stormed the national top twenty. However, by that time the success of the Shy FX and UK Apache collaboration had already been seen on an even larger scale with the infamous coupling of M Beat and General Levy on 'Incredible'. Coming out of the house of Renk Records the dub plate showed all the signs of blowing up when it hit the streets. But they could hardly have envisaged what would happen next.

Pre-sales demand was so high that shops were inundated with requests for the track. At one point heavy pirate airplay and soundsystem plugging turned the demand so high that one London Our Price Records store was forced to put a sign on its window declaring that 'Incredible' was not yet available to buy. In the event of its release, however, it hit the top ten instantly, subsequently heralding a renewed interest in Jungle from the media who immediately tagged the summer of 1994 to be the 'Summer of Jungle'.

'Incredible's' cry of 'Booyaka, booyaka' was everywhere, even getting adopted by Channel 4's Breakfast Show puppets, Zig and Zag. And by the time of that year's Notting Hill Carnival the 'Booyaka' call of Ragga-Jungle had taken over the streets of London, providing the overwhelming sound-track to city life with sub bass and Ragga chat belting out of super woofers everywhere.

Inevitably record labels started to commission Jungle remixes for everything. However, the major companies knew little about this scene and rather than doing any substantial research, which might have meant going to a Jungle rave, they simply rang up the studios for information. Never ones to look a gift horse in the mouth, the unscrupulous engineers at in-house production companies took up the Jungle version opportunity with the simple intent of making money from this latest remix opportunity.

Of course this wasn't universally true. Some labels, usually the Ragga independents, did know who was who in the scene and some superb mixes did appear. Take Buju Banton's 'Champion – Miami Mix', reworked for the Jungle raves to startling effect. Or then there was DJ Ron's remix of an unnamed Top Cat tune which had a rolling thirty-two-bar breakdown with a sub bass which seemed to come from the floor to make its way up your body until your legs, stomach, chest and head were all vibrating to the rhythm. To this was added a spine tingling display of toasting. The result: a wicked tune which always got rewound without fail.

For the Dark fraternity, however, the Ragga-Jungle takeover was, apart from the originals like Ron, Frost and Kane, very much a case of out-siders jumping on board and stealing their sound. Producers like Rob Playford looked down their noses at the scene declaring much of it to be devoid of any real creative talent. To him they were using a sound which he and his contemporaries had already dropped as far back as 1992. 'Personally after doing it for this amount of years it really got to me when people started doing the Ragga-Jungle thing,' sighs Playford. 'There were all of these people taking really obvious elements and sticking something even more obvious over it to try and make a pop record. The sound they were trying to copy was something very close to our hearts, very deep underground and it just pissed everybody off. I just felt like I had to get out of it at that point.'

Not surprisingly, in a move which found Rob Playford et al. finally denouncing the Jungle sound, the Dark elite moved back to their sonic laboratories to sculpt and shape the future – a sound which was to become increasingly known as Drum 'n' Bass. Not that this bothered the majority of the general public, though. After all, they still had the Jungle raves to go to.

JUNGLE RAVES

Until 1994 the hundred per cent Jungle raves had been relatively sporadic. In reality the numbers of people into the scene just weren't big enough to justify weekly events. Among the first of the Jungle raves was 'X – By Any Means Necessary' at the Brixton Academy. Featuring Micky Finn, Grooverider, Randall and Ron, the vibe was much darker than the happy atmosphere witnessed at the old style Hardcore raves. Indeed, according to one punter on the night there wasn't a single person smiling in the whole place. Dancing to this music was it seemed a serious business and the crowd took this to an extreme. But the atmosphere was still electric, with the music itself, rather than the drugs, carrying things.

Another of the early Jungle raves was perhaps more significant for the scene. 'Jungle Book' was the first time that pirate radio Kool FM had put on an event. By teaming up with another pirate they were able to promote the event over the airwaves around the clock. On the night approximately 5000 people turned up to a 2000-capacity venue. 'When we saw the turnout it was unbelievable!' recalls Kool FM mainstay Brockie. 'Everybody was there that was with this music, Jungle, something was happening. There were about 2000 people inside and out on the street there was about 3000 people. There were people ranging from eighteen to forty, all ages. The police had never seen anything like it.'

At a time when the authorities were hypersensitive to the underworld nature of rave culture, police intervention was simply inevitable. Scared by the sheer numbers of people on the streets, the police opted to use a softly softly approach of non-confrontation in order to move the crowds on. In both a defiant showdown against the authorities and a jubilant show of Junglist strength, the 3000 punters who had been refused entry just stood their ground, taunting and jeering the baton wielding boys in blue. Car soundsystems were turned on and tuned in to Kool FM, sending bass bin shock waves across the venue's pathways. A party was starting to happen out in the open as the streets gradually became lined with police vans, dogs and anti-riot troops. According to one eyewitness, the police moved in swinging their batons and striking out at anyone in an attempt to disperse the crowd. It was like the golden days of the warehouse party all over again. Old adversaries doing battle over the right to dance when and where people wanted.

The authorities may have succeeded in breaking up this particular party but they couldn't take away the fact that it was a momentous occasion. Proof positive that there was a growing army of Junglists surfing the underground vibe of the pirate stations. With this kind of demand the regular Jungle rave seemed just around the corner and in August 1993 the first 'Jungle Fever' took place.

An alliance between Kool FM and Ibiza Records, Jungle Fever aimed to give the Junglists exactly what they wanted. Powerful soundsystems, laser shows, a guarantee that all artists on the flyer would play and even more to the point, guaranteed payment in full to the artists. In an unprecedented move Jungle Fever also elected to employ their own security staff on the door. The ethos of the Jungle Fever promoters was quite simply one of mutual respect between promoters, artists and punters alike.

The very first Jungle Fever was almost a statement of intent to the whole scene. The venue was decorated like a graveyard with tombstones, coffins and Gothic statues in a move which attempted to exaggerate the dark mood of the times. The first of a series of themed events, it travelled from venue to venue around the capital and as far north as Milton Keynes, spelling out the simple fact that Jungle was here and growing at an amazing rate. 'Before us people were putting on events but they were afraid to label it Jungle,' exclaimed one of Jungle Fever's promoters in 1995. 'We wanted to present Jungle as it should be presented, and not water it down by mixing it with Garage, Techno and House. We said to our DJs this is Jungle Fever, you go ahead and take Jungle music to where it's going to go.'

At this point, of course, where Jungle was going was up. Jungle Fever proved to be a paradigm for other rave promoters and pretty soon after the first Jungle Fever rave the Roller Express in Edmonton opened its doors to the regular 'Jungle Splash' nights. An extremely important breeding ground for the burgeoning vocal Jungle movement, Roller Express boasted a steady diet of Jump Up tunes laced with live Ragga chatting and of course plenty of Jungled up soul divas.

It may have existed in a trading estate on the edge of London but Roller Express was massively popular both with audience and DJs alike. A typical line up was the one advertised on Saturday 2 July 1994: DJs Randall, Micky Finn, Brockie, Darren Jay, Jumping Jack Frost, Ray Keith and Hype, a VIP line up which echoed the better days at The Paradise Club.

Roller Express proved to be a turning point for two people who were to become inextricably linked with the scene soon after their first times there: Dave Stone and Cleveland Watkiss. For Stone it was an eye opener which was to change the direction of his company, SOUR Recordings. Until this point the label (and its formative DJ Only imprint) had looked towards releasing Hardcore records almost exclusively. To this end they'd already put out Bass Selective's 'Southern Fried Chicken' which featured future Junglists T-Power and Elizabeth Troy.

When Stone was played some Jungle stuff to consider releasing, he, like many others, simply didn't get it. There was no kick drum, so how could people dance to it? But he was interested enough to check out the Jungle raves. Of these life-changing events, Stone says:

I went out with Shy FX to a few of the raves down in Edmonton and I really liked what I saw. I really liked the vibe in these places. It was different from the Hardcore. There was like a fifty/fifty mix of black and white but you could really feel the black influence with the Ragga samples and the Reggae bass lines. The DJs who were mainly black were pushing a real skanking feel which I instantly understood because I was into Reggae. It was the bass line which gave the half time dance rhythm, not the bpms. It quickly made sense to me in the context of the rave.

Soon afterwards Stone sanctioned the release of T-Power's extremely experimental 'Lipsing Jamring' and Shy FX's 'Gangster Kid'. He went on to form SOUR Records as a home for the entire spectrum of the sound of Drum 'n' Bass – from Ragga-Jungle to Ambient.

For Cleveland Watkiss the discovery of the Jungle vibe was far more accidental. A stalwart of the Jazz scene thanks to his days with the Jazz Warriors, he'd had very little to do with the rave scene. His days of clubbing were far more based around Giles Peterson's Dingwalls Jazz floorshakers. Having lived in London's East End for a number of years, however, the Jungle buzz had grown up all around him and it wasn't long before the rave beckoned. He enthuses:

My first Roller Express event is when Jungle actually clicked for me. I'd been listening to this stuff for maybe two years but I'd never been to these raves and as soon as I did the music just grabbed me, man. I hadn't heard anything like this since I first heard Be-bop. I knew immediately I was going to be involved. I had been hanging around the Jazz scene and people in that world, man, they were like 'What are you doing listening to that shit'. But the Jungle scene is a real integration of cultures on a level which I've never really experienced before. It's a product of multiculturalism.

As Jungle raves flourished in early 1994 so too did the regular club nights in London. Already a haunt for the Junglists, the Astoria's 'Sunday Roast' (returning from a spell at Linford Film Studios) encapsulated the vibe. Heavy and hard, beats rumbling at a furious rate with a predominantly black crowd soaking it up, rolling it and blowing Jungle's smoke back into the room. Everton, the promoter of Roast, explained to *True Magazine* at the time exactly why the club was so important for a scene continually affected by the prejudices of London's clubland. 'It was difficult for a black man to get into West End clubs then. Roast broke down some barriers,' he argued.

In a move which seemed to take Everton's example to heart, the line up of London clubs devoting nights to Jungle soon increased. 'Ah . . . London Sumtin'' alternated between Samantha's on Burlington Street and the Vox in Brixton, and featured residencies from Brockie, Brian G, DJ Ron, Trace and Stretch with regular MCs 5-O and Det. 'Thunder and Joy' took over Raw on Tottenham Court Road every other Sunday. A basement set six floors beneath the YMCA, Raw offered the best in subterranean clubbing. 'Thunder and Joy' brought together people from all over the south east of England, attracted by its booming 24K soundsystem and full on line up which included Rap, Nicky

Blackmarket, Darren Jay, Brockie, SL and the Demolition Kru.

Meanwhile, the unlikely surroundings of the Marquee Club opened its doors to what was described as a night from 'the original dub trance Junglists'. Called 'Electrybe', the Marquee nights were aimed more specifically at Drum 'n' Bass, the melodic side of Jungle which had started to emerge. However, this was still very much in its infancy and in the majority of the capital's clubs the mood was still tough.

Nowhere was this more evident than in south east London. A definite no-go area for the north London-centric major media, the south east had gained a reputation for its bad attitude. But it had also become known for some wicked club nights like Peckham Rye's infamous 'Lazerdrome'. Perhaps as well known as north London's A.W.O.L., Lazerdrome would boast the same DJs; however, the atmosphere was totally different. If a divide was ever evident in the Jungle scene at this time, then it was here – a north/south divide, that is.

The Lazerdrome was Ragga-Jungle central. Tapping into the huge West Indian and Jamaican populations of the area, the club seemed to develop an exaggerated bad boy image. An outward statement of pride, this was a south east London thing, a place where only the toughest survive.

The Lazerdrome proved to be the perfect setting for Desert Storm, the Jungle offshoot of Jarvis Sandy's Biology promotions. Desert Storm put on two events in Peckham, 'The Lick' and 'Simple Tings'. And while both were marred by violence, they proved to be stunning nights with DJ sets coming from the Jungle vanguard; Grooverider, Hype, Randall, Jumping Jack Frost, Ray Keith, DJ Rap, Cool Hand Flex, DJ SS and Tonic all tearing up the dancefloor with their ruffneck beats.

Perhaps the most noticeable thing about the Jungle raves, apart from the music itself, was the style. Quite the opposite to the dress down utilitarian wear which had dominated the rave scene, Junglism was all about an overtly sexual image. The music itself tapped into a raw sexuality with a half time sub bass which aimed straight at the pelvis, and the fashion naturally sought to highlight this. Women dressed in the smallest shorts imaginable. Made from tight Lycra plastic, these shorts gained the name 'batty riders'. Legs would be adorned in thigh length leather boots while leather waistcoats were worn on top. The colours: black and gold.

If the order of the day for the women was tight, small and revealing then the dancing left little to the imagination. Employing a style derived from bogling, a Ragga dance which is totally sexual, women would thrust their pelvises in time with the breaks, interspersing this movement with slower pelvic gyrations to emphasise the bass lines. Dancing in packs down the front of the hall, the women would present a scene of 'come and get us boys' sexuality while sticking together in the safety of group numbers.

The men on the other hand would just stand and stare, occasionally venturing to the edge of the girl posse, swaying to the sensual beat of the music. However, the guys were putting on their own display of sexual attraction. Dressed to kill in (often copied) designer chic they wore the sharp styles of Versace, Moschino and Armani. Theirs was a far more predatorial style, the streetwise look of a bad boy on the prowl. They'd be far more likely to stand around checking people out than actually dancing. When movement did break out among the men, it invariably took shape as an on the spot skanking style or simply bursts of jumping up and down on the spot.

The crowds were also extremely loud. To them the Jungle rave wasn't just about dancing or picking up members of the opposite sex, it was about complete involvement. An extension of the total commitment attitude central to the Junglist psychology, the crowd would demand rewinds and when the MC shouted for them to make some noise the cacophony was almost deafening. Appreciation was further expressed by people waving lighters set to maximum flame in the air. All a part of the wild sense of euphoria which gripped these events.

In late 1994 James Style of the *Independent* noted with apparent amazement the energy and volume of the Jungle crowd: 'The crowd are not just dancing – they are letting off fog-horns, whistles and holding lighters in the air'. He described the sound as being 'to music what Mortal Kombat is to video games. Aggressive, violent, but totally compulsive.'

Similar stories were run in almost every style and music magazine from *Select* (the bastion of guitar based indie pop) to *GQ*. The broadsheets also took on a fresh and positive view of Jungle with features appearing in the *Guardian* and the *Independent*. It was as if the media had facilitated a hypocritical about turn and jumped on the high rolling Jungle gravy train, temporarily forgetting the previous rejection of the scene. Even MTV started to interview the stars of the Jungle scene. The reality, however, was that a number of people within the greater media had stayed with the underground culture, but it had taken a top twenty hit to convince the gatekeeping forces of editorial departments and the decision makers 'upstairs' that Jungle was a very real force.

However, music magazine editors caught up in the bright lights and coke lines of the emerging House and Techno hegemony had been found guilty of being asleep at the wheel, whilst the most important UK phenomenon in twenty years had been unfolding under their very noses. In a mad rush to cover Jungle they went straight to General Levy and the MCs.

In a scene where the producers and DJs preferred to be unseen faces in the shadows, the space was wide open for the MCs to take over as the personalities of Jungle. These were the people whose voices were carried across the soundsystems of the clubs and the airwaves of the pirate stations. The mouthpieces behind endless streams of psycho babble, shout outs and buzz phrases. And for many, they were the catalysts who translated the energy of the music into the language of the rave.

Leaning out towards the crowd, mics firmly to lips, the MCs would ride the ebb and flow of the rolling beats, working the audience with their lyrical dexterity, pushing the vibe to intensified crescendos while spreading their patter across the smoother passages. The MCs carried the credo to the audience, boasting about the Jungle massive and supplying a stronger sense of identity.

Each different personality on the mic would push their own catchphrase. MC Moose would holler his feelings that Jungle was 'like malaria, it's contagious', while 5-O pushed his own version of Jungle's cultural significance describing the movement as 'the biggest thing since England won the World Cup'.

If Jungle seemed to have an at times overly high self esteem then surely it came from the MCs and their irrepressible excitement, something which outsiders would see as arrogance but insiders would define as street attitude. With Jungle these rebels had a very real cause to fight for and the MCs were the unelected spokesmen.

Jungle's adoption of the MC from the Reggae soundsystem and the Hip Hop block jam tied the scene even deeper into a sense of history. Little surprise then that every man, woman and dog wanted to emulate the MCs they'd grown up listening to. After all they'd been singing along to these Reggae plates and Hip Hop tunes for years, just how difficult could it be?

In the event MCing proved to be an art form that few could master. DJs would increasingly complain that the MCs' egos took over as soon as their words were amplified. The power of hearing themselves over the soundsystem would open the sluice gates on an unending barrage of words, riding over the beats and crushing the vibe of the music. Quite simply, once they'd started they couldn't be stopped. Furthermore the increasing celebrity status of the MCs, with some getting a higher billing on the flyers than the DJs themselves, created a very real friction.

For the DJs the music was paramount. Although individuals were allowed a certain underground celebrity status, no DJ was more important than the scene that they were representing. As such no individual could take any credit for things. Little more than an unwritten rule, it was, however, accepted by everyone involved out of respect for the scene they'd stuck with, protected and subsequently nurtured.

These workings (or 'runnings' as they are often referred to) were the glue which held things together. However, with MCs slowly being elevated as the 'chosen spokespeople', the media were finally able to cover this sound while adhering to a star system that Jungle had previously universally rejected.

Until this point most publications were shy of any movement without its figureheads. Sure Fabio, Grooverider and their ilk were able to pack out the raves and bootleggers could sell enormous quantities of mix tapes bearing their names, but as individuals they resolutely refused to play the media celebrity game. Suddenly the MCs provided faces for the photos and quotes for the articles. The ripples of dissatisfaction spread throughout the scene, with many DJs openly condemning the acts of these new stars of the microphone. 'MCs', according to Dego McFarlane, 'are people who chat over records to help with the vibe so people can have a good time in a club, that's it, full stop. I mean if I want vocals on a track I put them there. But some MCs started thinking they were more important than everyone else and because a lot of producers aren't interested in talking to the press the MCs started coming forward.'

Indeed the tension was starting to show increasingly in the clubs with MCs flexing their self proclaimed importance at every opportunity. More and more MCs would call a rewind of a tune, not because the crowd had shouted for it but because they personally liked it.

DJs complained bitterly. Microphones would be unplugged in disgust and some DJs would only allow their own chosen MCing partner on the mic. As a result many of Jungle's partnerships started to emerge: DJs teaming up with MCs who understood about the spaces in the music quickly rising to the top of the pack. To Cleveland Watkiss, better known as the Metalheads MC, this understanding of space is paramount to a good vocal delivery: 'If I'm going to chat or MC on top of someone else's music I have to respect it first. The thing is you've got your MCs and they've just written some bad lyrics and they want to run them, which is understandable. But you have to find the right space first.'

Unfortunately not all of Jungle's MCs had Watkiss's humility or natural musical ability and as such the tensions between vocalist and DJ just grew. By 1995 the only MCs still getting major respect from the scene were ones who believed in space and musicality over and beyond their own individual egos. People like Conrad, Watkiss, MC Det, 5-0, Navigator and GQ who remained intent on pushing the scene forward.

RECOMMENDED LISTENING

'Limb by Limb' – Cutty Ranks (Suburban Base)

'Unity' – Remarc (Kemet)

'RIP' – Remarc (Suburban Base)

'Armed and Dangerous' – Cutty Ranks (Fashion)

'The Burial' – Leviticus (Ffrr)

'Tear Down (Da Whole Place) – Dillinja (white)

'So Simple' – Potential Bad Boy featuring MC Det (SOUR)

'Incredible' – M Beat featuring General Levy (Renk)

'Original Nuttah' – UK Apachi with Shy FX (SOUR)

'Warning' – Ibiza (white)

'Code Red' – Conquering Lion (X-Project)

'28 Gun Bad Boy' – Various (Juicebox)

'Gangsta Kid' – Shy FX (SOUR)

'Wheel Up' – Lion Man (Lucky Spin)

'Runnin' For Years' – L Double Presents Liccle D (Little Rollers)

'Connections' – Skenk Gee (Suburban Base)

'Ruffest Gunark' – Top Cat Meets DJ Rap (Fashion)

5: ABOVE THE LAW

THE BUSINESS INFRASTRUCTURE

During Jungle's years outside the media spotlight the scene developed its own hugely independent business infrastructure. With its own record labels, distribution networks, shops, pirate radio stations and fanzines the scene was able to sustain itself with a degree of autonomy away from the mainstream.

Through the ease with which records could be independently manufactured, record labels sprang up all over the place. However, only the most organised survived the earliest times. Dan Donnelly's Suburban Bass grew out of Hardcore and embraced Jungle as it developed, as did Reinforced Records, Moving Shadow and De Underground. Paul Chambers's Ibiza set up backed the scene with a series of compilations on Jumping and Pumping Records. Called 'Jungle Tekno', they were to be important factors in the shaping of the scene. As the scene grew, seemingly every DJ set up their own label to put out the kind of tracks they wanted to DJ with.

Essential to the labels were the shops. Specialist shops had grown out of the Hardcore sound and they existed on the outside of the mainstream, in a way which echoed the independence of the Reggae specialist shops which had serviced their own market for many years. Places like Ibiza in Dalston, Jungle Fever in Clapton, De Underground in Forest Gate, Vinyl Mania in Ealing, Renk in Tottenham, Music Power in Ilford, Boogie Times in Romford, Wax and The Big Apple in Croydon, Jus' Dance in Eltham and the central London stores like Lucky Spin, Unity, Razor, Blackmarket and

Section 5; the list was endless for London alone. Cities throughout the country had their equivalents, all of which became important meeting grounds for the different crews which made up the nascent scene.

Around the shops emerged a distribution network. Working from the backs of vans the underground distributors were reminiscent of the days when underground labels would take boxes of records around the shops trying to sell them on spec. By the time the rave scene had taken hold it had turned into a far more professional concern, with van salesmen representing a vast selection of labels. Jungle's main distributor was Vinyl Distribution in Reading which worked alongside their Basement Records shop.

The most important source of promotion for the records came through the pirate radio stations. An integral part of the pre-legal rave scene, the position of the pirates as champions of the underground was paramount. The pirates were the ones who held the information, they had the power and even more to the point they were playing the music as it happened and were not months behind, like the legal stations. 'They literally are the backbone of the underground,' enthuses A Guy Called Gerald, whose main exposure to the pirates came with his trips to London. 'Without them I don't think half of the raves like Jungle Fever, Champagne Slash and A.W.O.L. and all them early things would have been anywhere near successful. Nobody would've known.'

Pirate station organisers held an extreme suspicion of anyone not directly connected. If caught in the act of transmitting illegally the organiser invariably received major fines and of course all equipment was confiscated. As a result the pirates generated an incredible buzz of excitement, always at least two steps ahead of the law. Hopefully.

Nicky Blackmarket was a mainstay of the London pirates, with an involvement which dates back to the pre-rave warehouse days. As such he's grown with them. Before giving his own personal history lesson, he explains:

To me pirate radio has been very important in all of the dance music scenes, but especially Jungle. At first you had LWR. Horizon, Invicta, Solar, JFM and all the dance DJs now come from that. Then the rave thing came big and you had Fantasy, Centreforce and then they sort of stopped. Next came the new breed of Rave, the Hardcore stations like Pulse FM. I was one of the original DJs on Pulse in '90, '91, when the Rave thing was blowing up you know. From there you had Rush which is where you had the beginning of Kool FM.

The single most important pirate station in Jungle is Kool FM. Since its beginnings it has always charted each change on the scene, using its ability to get across to thousands of people at a time to publicise the Jungle raves. Indeed so important was Kool that breaking a record depended on getting airplay on one of its shows. For the DJs like Nicky Blackmarket the shows allowed them to react to what was going on in the raves much more quickly. He explains:

You play a tune one night and there's a right buzz about it, it's just tearin' the place. So you take the same tune to your next show which might be that morning and you know it's got a vibe. Sometimes I just get to Kool straight after a gig, or straight out of bed. I've been up there in my pyjamas before. I hadn't slept because of doing raves and I'd just think, 'What the fuck'. I'll just roll in and do it. It means I'm still on a buzz from the gig.

Pirate stations were notoriously rough and ready. Transmissions would be regularly broken as the pirates temporarily closed down. When up and running the DJs would play the most up front stuff possible as MCs shouted out to the various crews. The sound was raw, an energetic, community-minded force which played the music of the street, trampling legal radio shows into the ground.

The DJs and MCs too inspired their own business offshoots in the shape of DJ agencies. Running the DJs' bookings to the optimum ensured that not only did the DJs and MCs remain busy but also that the scene was well serviced. Indeed the agencies can be seen as being imperative to the growth of the scene with Groove Connection, Unique, UMC and Jungle Fever playing a central role.

The pirates may have been the fastest way of communicating information but working alongside them were the fanzines like Bristol's *Knowledge* and the south coast's *Atmosphere*. Put together via home use desktop publishing kits, they represented a quick and effective way of spreading the word without ever relying on the slow mechanisms of the established press.

With such a strong business infrastructure in place, the Jungle scene was able to push forward while still keeping control. The Punk Rock scene of the late 1970s may have pioneered the independent label but no one had ever experienced the level of independence and autonomy that was enjoyed by the Jungle network.

THE TECHNOLOGY

Of course Jungle would never have existed if it hadn't have been for the technology behind it. However, unlike the Rock scene which requires vast amounts of equipment for recording, Jungle's needs are relatively simple.

Originally, Jungle was made up of digitised data culled from older recordings, videos and CD sound collections and transposed on to the sampler. The most popular make of sampler was the Akai S-950 which was then linked with a sequencing package like Cubase, C Lab or Creator which took the raw sample and allowed you to arrange the samples into rhythmic 'loops' in technologically enhanced versions of the Breakbeat. The beauty of Cubase for the Junglist however was the ease with which it could be copied. 'The programmers had no idea their software was going to get rinsed out,' laughs Cleveland Watkiss. 'At the time they just imagined it being a tool for the Rock musician or something like a karaoke thing. Imagine what they would have done if they'd realised that this music was going to come along.'

It was a sentiment backed up by the entire scene. Without Akai and Cubase Jungle would never have taken its shape; a form which was built around the manipulation of a four bar break. In an interview with Tim Barr, Rob Playford recalled the extremes he would go to to make a track sound interesting by cutting up the breaks into smaller sections. 'We used to use Hip Hop breaks on our tracks to create a better groove rather than just having a straight four/four of a drum machine,' explained Playford of the techniques employed by him, Sean O'Keefe and Simon Colbrooke for their 2 Bad Mice material, 'but on "Waremouse", instead of just running loops, we triggered the breaks. We'd let the loop run for one and a half beats and then re-trigger it so it sounded like we had a totally new break.'

It was a sound which went completely against the design of the package. This was the pioneering attitude which lay at the heart of the best programming techniques. To take the software and push the sound through the ringer backwards, just to see what it could do.

On one such sonic excursion into the unknown, A Guy Called Gerald discovered fresh potential in the S-950 sampler through the separation of sound across two band widths, a trick which can be heard on a number of his earlier tracks. He told *The Wire*:

There's two separate bands: one is the main band that goes forwards and then there's another one which goes forwards and backwards. So I started running some loops through that and it sounded really funky. I'd have something going forwards for a beat and then reversing for the other beat. You could create a sound that you couldn't quite recognise because it would be going backwards . . . As well as sequencing drums you could actually take a break and totally delve into it, process some of the sounds, filter things out of it, reverse loops, have some loops going forwards, some going backwards, just getting more rhythmic.

It was an art form which took the musician through so many twists and turns that the resulting music seemed beyond people's wildest dreams. It was space music, found through a naive need to take things apart and then reconstruct them in an alternative sonic form which was subsequently launched on an ether bound trip on to the dancefloors and into the imagination.

As the scene progressed so too did the equipment required. For Rob Playford, whose work with Goldie took Jungle to new extremes of production techniques, the growth of the scene can be seen through the equipment used. His own beginnings were with a Yamaha DX7, an Atari PC and a shareware sequencer called Superconductor. It was through the inclusion of the Akai S-950 sampler that he was able to make his first records. However, by the time he had started working on Goldie's later material which was to become his first album, he had upgraded his PC to a Macintosh running Logic Audio. It was like exchanging a Ford Capri for a BMW Series 3. 'The thing about this technology is that it's like getting into a very fast car', says Goldie, 'like a Ferrari or something. But you're not driving it the way the manual says you're supposed to, you're joyriding. And that's what we do. We're joyriding technology, pushing it to the edge.'

An important feature of the Jungle movement has been the use of very up front and exclusive dub plates. As a result the cutting rooms where these plates are made have become a hotbed of fresh sound, the places where DJs meet, checking out who's boasting which exclusives. Perhaps the single most important cutting room in Jungle since the very beginning has been Music House. Set up in 1984 by Chris Hanson of late 1970s Reggae band Black Slate, Music House specialised in mastering dub plates for the London Dub Soundsystems. However, with the arrival of Jungle business boomed as the dub plates became ever more popular in the scene.

As time progressed Music House saw a continued meeting of the most important people in the scene. And, as the DJs all heard the new sounds coming through within the confines of the cutting room, they developed a consensus of what was to represent the next cutting edge, the next step forward.

RECOMMENDED LISTENING

All various artists compilations

'Platinum Breaks' (Metalheads)

'Grooverider Presents the Prototype Years' (Prototype)

'Bukem Presents Logical Progression' (Ffrr)

'Enforcers – Above The Law' (Reinforced)

'Intelligent Minds of Jungle' (Reinforced)

'Classics' (V Recordings)

'Music Box' (Full Cycle)

'Revolutionary Generation' (Creative Wax/Moving Shadow)

'Torque' (No U-Turn)

'Techsteppin'' (Emotif)

'Danger UED' (Emotif)

'Routes From The Jungle' (Virgin)

'Suspect Package' (Hard Leaders)

'Hidden Rooms' (Certificate 18)

'Junglized' (Selector)

'Total Science Vol 1 & 2' (Black Market)

'Artcore Vol 1 & 3' (React)

'Pure Rollers' (Breakdown)

'Still Smokin'' (Ganja Records)

6: SHADOW BOXING

THE JUNGLE/DRUM 'N' BASS SPLIT

Perhaps the most important year for the development of Jungle was 1994. With popularity increasing by the day, the underground forces of the scene were being made to face up to the very real threat of an encroaching media, and the ever lustful eye of the major record industry on the lookout for the 'next big thing'. A pivotal time, the moves made in these twelve months could either make or break the scene.

The Jungle fraternity may have created a subterranean business structure tailored to meet the limited needs of an audience which was largely London based (although there were important Junglist pockets developing all around the country, most notably Bristol, Coventry and the south coast), but the question still remained as to whether the 'runnings' were tight enough to compete on a much wider level. And whether the scene's players would be respected enough to call the shots in dealings with major labels.

However, a far more immediate concern was the growing interest of the wider media. Not only had the printed media increased its coverage on what they considered to represent Jungle, but both TV and radio had started to try and represent the scene. The potential for the promotion of the wrong people was huge as the media sought to access the easiest, most newsworthy artists.

With the existing Jungle media of underground fanzines and pirate stations only a very limited audience was being accessed. Subsequently the true word of Jungle remained localised to the circulations of the fanzines and the transmitter radius of the pirates. A subterranean distribution of mix tapes may well have reached a wider audience but still their impact was minimal. With the greater media's growing interest came a very real potential for both misrepresentation and individuals 'selling out'. Used to dealing with industry on a very localised level, the Jungle scene was now looking directly into the snapping jaws of major league companies like MTV. Jungle's main faces took on a defensive stance of non-cooperation. MTV, along with the rest of the national media, had never been interested before and the scene had grown to huge proportions without their help. Indeed, whether Jungle was covered by the national press, radio and TV or not was considered irrelevant. There would, the Junglists thought, always be a Jungle scene with or without outside involvement, so they simply didn't need anyone else.

Beamed across the whole of Europe, MTV's audience potential was staggering in comparison to the figures Jungle was used to dealing with. The station's underground dance music show Partyzone had attempted to include Jungle among the featured styles from very early on. However, producer James Hyman and his team were faced with the immediate problem of suspicion from the scene. Despite being the first TV show to offer the space to the Jungle movement, the Junglists were extremely reluctant to be seen to be getting into bed with this corporate station.

This showed one of the very many dilemmas which were starting to face the Jungle front line. While wanting to remain true to both their underground roots and their 'outsider' ideology, they also had a desire to spread the word. There were obvious economic concerns. Many of the Jungle DJs had been around for years and naturally wanted to earn money from the work they were doing. People now had families to support, subsequently what was OK when they were youths in the Acid House days was certainly not OK now; it was a different game entirely.

Similarly the record labels that the DJs all seemed to be setting up needed a wider public to purchase their product. A dichotomy presented itself. Media attention was unavoidable for a while, so the Jungle fraternity had to take a greater control over how the media were going to represent the scene. It was the only way they could keep the underground vibe alive.

'The papers and magazines have to sell copies so the journalists go straight for sensationalism,' explains Goldie. 'It's the way of the business. TV and radio are the same really, it's the way it works, so we had to make sure the media talked about the right people. Otherwise they'd just go for anyone that fitted the bill.'

Happily for the Jungle scene's inner sanctum of original DJs and producers, Hyman's love of the Jungle sound wasn't a recent one. He'd followed the scene closely since the Hardcore days so when he did cover things he went straight to its creative core. Features on Reinforced Records, Goldie and X-Project were shown. And when the Partyzone covered General Levy who had scored a top twenty Ragga-Jungle hit with 'Incredible', it remained within the context of Ragga as opposed to presenting him as an important face in Jungle as many others had done. With James Hyman and show presenter Simone Angel, the Jungle scene had found very real allies who were prepared to take the time and effort to understand this very precious musical development.

Not that this prevented Rebel MC from sticking the boot in a little on an edition of the show in August 1994. On set with Jumping Jack Frost and MC 5-0 (the rest of the X-Project triumvirate who were promoting their killer Conquering Lion track 'Code Red'), Rebel expressed his concerns about MTV's late discovery of Jungle. He complains:

Last year MTV didn't want to know about Jungle. We were busting some bad tunes before but it's only now you ask X-Project to talk about it. And you think you're being revolutionary . . . MTV, the way the shows are televised, is supposed to be all about bustin' the status quo. So tell me why didn't they do stuff about us two years ago. MTV will report on stuff which is in LA's back garden but when the thing is in your own back garden you ignore it. Suddenly Jungle is like tearing down the place and now, in 1994, you're like 'get them on the show'.

Despite Simone's attempts to explain the slow workings of corporate machinery Rebel remained unappeased, going on to boast that 'Jungle don't need MTV anyway'. Within the Jungle fraternity it would seem there was a very real feeling of resentment about the cold shoulder they'd been shown over the past couple of years. These interviews suddenly gave Jungle the chance to express its anger in no uncertain terms. Ironically Partyzone had done what it could to represent the scene. The main problem lay in the fact that Partyzone was a video-based show and the Jungle scene simply wasn't producing videos at first. However, Hyman and team had long included Jungle records in their recommended lists. It wasn't until the Junglists had started to produce good quality videos that Partyzone were fully able to promote the scene. In turn, promotional videos were extremely low on the list of concerns of a scene who had no need to sell themselves on TV. After all, as Rebel said, they didn't need MTV.

This of course was true. If the Jungle scene was happy to remain selling only 500 records per release and to continue preaching to the converted, then Jungle had no need for MTV . . . or indeed any of the major media. In reality, however, many of the Junglist front line, most notably Goldie, were already in talks with the major record labels. And media whoring was almost a prerequisite of signing in to the music industry's premier league.

The media development which received the most attention among the Junglists, however, was the announcement that London's Kiss FM was to run a weekly Jungle show. As an ex-pirate, Kiss was seen by many as the radio station which 'sold out' the underground, its involvement with the dance scene now merely a pawn for the major industry's radio pluggers. Kiss was the station where the crossover dance hits were played first and as such they became a very important element in the industry's marketing campaigns.

Kiss FM sold itself to the listening public as having an ear on the underground, representing real sounds. However, like *Mixmag* they'd largely championed the commercial House stuff over anything else. Sure they had specialist shows to cater for the Jazz, Hip Hop and R&B fraternities but since their inception they'd almost completely ignored the post-Hardcore developments in Breakbeat. Indeed at times it seemed like Kiss were adopting similar exclusion policies as the clubs, with Junglist records being completely ignored. Rob Playford came up against Kiss FM's unwritten no Jungle policy when one of Moving Shadow's releases was top of the Kiss 100 chart yet it still wasn't getting air play:

I can't remember which track it was now but I do know they refused to play it. I just kept phoning them up about it and they'd be saying 'What record do you mean?' and I'd just shout at them that it was top of their fucking charts and still they'd deny its existence. Or they'd say that they hadn't received it when we'd actually sent them loads of copies, even biked some over to make sure. It was obvious they just hated all of our stuff. Then suddenly Jungle was trendy and they loved our stuff, couldn't get enough of us. It was so strange, you know. Out of favour one week and then flavour of the month the next. I just thought, 'Haven't these people got brains of their own? Obviously not'.

Like everyone else Kiss FM had been caught napping over the growth of Jungle. Jungle's listeners were apparently not the kind of people who would tune into the legal transmissions of Kiss when they had their own, rough and ready pirates. It is also possible that Kiss, like so many others, had adopted a policy of 'ignore them and they might go away'.

But Jungle refused to die; it just got stronger instead and eventually Kiss FM had to cave in to demand. Not only from the listeners but also from their Head of Specialist Programmes, Wilber Wilberforce, who'd been into Jungle long enough to know how special it was.

Wilberforce remembers a different story, however. Kiss FM, he maintains, had long been interested in doing a Jungle show. The problem was how exactly to approach it, the militant democracy of the scene making it almost impossible to single out any individual as a representative. 'In the end I selected the DJs via a process of elimination,' he explains. However, that process wasn't simply a case of tuning into the pirates, something which Wilberforce did regularly anyway. He also needed to discover which DJs could have a professional enough approach to fit into the very exacting demands of Kiss FM. There was a world of difference between pirate radio and the commercial transmissions of the legal station, so Wilberforce invited DJs to play the weekly specialist slot 'Give it Up'. 'It gave me the chance to see which DJs were best suited to radio,' he says of the difficult task he'd set himself. 'I think they thought that I was just going to select one DJ to do the Jungle show so a lot of the DJs apparently weren't happy about things. But I thought that it would be wrong, especially when the scene was so varied.'

By the time the show became a reality Wilberforce had decided that the best way to deal with the tangled politics of the subculture was to put the DJs on rotation with the first slots going to Jumping Jack Frost, DJ Randall, Kenny Ken and DJ Hype.

The immediate runaway success of the Wednesday night two hour slot threw straight out of the window any doubts Kiss might have had about Jungle. The listening figures went through the roof with the listeners displaying a rare level of feedback. Unlike Kiss's other shows which received a trickle of mail, the Jungle show was sent letters by the sackful. The Junglists had always been extremely active in their own scene and the Kiss show wasn't going to be an exception. 'It's quite rare for a listener to write in and say "I always listen to the show and I love every track",' says Lorna Clarke of Kiss FM. 'But we get people listening to the show and writing two weeks before the DJs are on, and in some cases before we've even confirmed their appearance, saying "I know you've got Rap or Fabio and Grooverider on or whoever coming on, tell us the dates that they're going to be doing it so we can be sure to listen".'

This kind of response was literally unprecedented for Kiss. Consequently they decided to deal with the obvious demand by launching a second show on a Friday night. Although Wilberforce had initially toyed with the idea of giving the show to L. T. J. Bukem, a DJ who was noted for his laid back take on Jungle, he eventually decided that the DJ rotation approach would remain intact. However, this time it involved only two DJs, Fabio and Grooverider. With pride at securing the signatures of this legendary duo, Wilberforce says:

We got Fabio and Grooverider in. Initially the idea was to get Bukem for Friday but I just thought it would cause too much friction with other DJs. It would have caused a lot of bickering so I looked towards the people that everyone called the originators, Fabio and Groove. They were the best choice in the end anyway, not only because the scene was happy but also because they were playing the widest style of music.

The increased popularity of the Jungle shows more than justified Wilberforce's belief in the music's ability to translate to commercial radio.

And, although Jungle had already been a regular feature of dance shows around the country, like Mark Spivey's 'Get on the Good Foot' on Nottingham's Trent FM, it was Kiss FM who really showed that Jungle was the way forward. And when the Manchester franchise of Kiss was launched as Kiss 102, a Jungle show was an immediate feature in the programming schedule.

As the increased interest from the printed media, MTV's coverage and the specialist shows on Kiss reached ever wider audiences, Jungle shows could no longer be seen as simply an underground sound. It was so much more than that, the beliefs of its long time stalwarts now truly paying off.

Despite the few TV and radio producers and magazine journalists who were prepared to take the time to understand the scene, the rest of the media were proving to be less than respectful. By the time of General Levy's 'Incredible', the so-called 'Summer of Jungle' and August 1994's Notting Hill Carnival rocking to the Jungle vibe, the story-hungry magazines had run straight towards the Ragga-Jungle crossover for printable copy. The Junglists were far too moody to supply good quotes, although General Levy loved to talk. And, since he promised good copy as well as a top twenty hit, he was quickly elected as the chosen face of Jungle.

THE COMMITTEE

With the spotlight of the media came increasing disagreements within the scene's various factions. Cracks started to appear as promoters attempted to sabotage each other's Jungle raves and the DJs themselves became caught up in a fight to keep the original sentiments of Rave alive. The multitude of crews within the greater family of Jungle increasingly jostled for a stronger power base within the runnings. The newcomers wanted control.

Things were in fact increasingly out of control as far as the DJs and producers could see, a situation which was being aggravated by the increased growth of Ragga-Jungle whose MCs and vocalists were seen as stars within their own scene.

By the summer of 1994 things were at boiling point. Jungle had entered the charts thanks to records produced by relative newcomers to the scene. As Top of the Pops beckoned, journalists queued up and the original movers from the days of Dark were forced to watch as their sound was taken away from them. A word perfect repeat of Acid House and Hardcore seemed to be occurring as the jaws of major industry started snapping at Jungle's heels. Rob Playford explains: 'It was like we'd had years of people asking what sort of music we'd been doing. We'd explain it to them and then suddenly the same people would be going, "Yeah, I heard some of that stuff you're doing on Radio 1, it's rubbish". It was like, "Fucking hell, they're trying to take it away from us", and people started to associate us with that rubbish.'

If this wasn't enough General Levy let the success of 'Incredible' go straight to his mouth. In an interview in *The Face* he committed the cardinal sin and claimed to be running Jungle. 'I *run* Jungle at the moment', he was reported to have said. 'I came along and bigged up Jungle. I took it national. People might say I came along and jumped on the bandwagon but my track "Heat" was being battered at Junglist raves. I didn't mind because I wasn't raving at those raves. All I did was ring up Renk Records and suggest they use my live vocal instead. Now I'm running Jungle. Big time.'

It proved to be the final straw and a chasm appeared between the Johnny come lately Ragga-Junglists and the old skool Darkcore/Drum 'n' Bass heads. It was clear that the real originals would have to take a very real control over things if they were to stop the collapse of their scene. The wrong people had come to represent the Jungle sound and in a huge show of unity the real originals got together and formed the Jungle Committee.

Instigated by Rebel MC, the committee (or council as they would sometimes refer to themselves), was intended to act as a mediator between the scene and the media. A united front against the workings of the greater music industry, Fabio, Grooverider, Goldie and A Guy Called Gerald were just a few of the names allegedly involved in these secret monthly meetings. However, many others refused to be a part of what they saw as a childish act of paranoia, born more out of jealousy of the money Levy was purported to have made rather than any concern for the scene.

In horror at the very thought of the committee, Dego McFarlane exclaims:

What a pile of shite. We had no involvement in it. Fucking kids. Boys all talking shit. I bet they must feel embarrassed looking back at that now. And if they don't they're arseholes. I mean, what music scene forms a committee? I know Hip Hop had to because of the gang wars and the East Coast/West Coast stuff. They had to have emergency meetings, it was life or death man. But Drum 'n' Bass? If they'd had meetings about how we could further ourselves and keep control then maybe that would have been a good thing. That's what they pretend it was about, but it was about jealousy. I mean, what music actually has meetings about an MC shooting his mouth off? A lot of green-eyed people were involved in that committee. Jealous about how much money Levy was making. And you know what? I hope he made a fortune out of that record because I know what it's like to be a musician who's not making any money. First time anyone started to get any recognition and then this thing happened. It was all bollocks, I'm so happy I wasn't involved.

McFarlane's refusal to get involved with the committee was significant. As a key player in the early days of Darkcore with Reinforced Records the participation of Dego and partners Mark, Gus and Ian would protect much of the credibility of a council which was trying to gain control of the current events. The committee was established around a sense of history and much of their argument against the flurry of Ragga MC top twenty hits was based around their relatively recent conversion to Jungle. The very nature of which dictated that, if the committee was to have any authenticity, the scene's old guard had to be involved. Reinforced's decision to avoid the meetings instantly pointed at a fundamental weakness in the committee's infrastructure.

However, those that did attend the meetings were powerful enough to have an immediate effect on some matters which were close to their hearts. Matters which may seem petty now but at the time created an enormous amount of tension. It was clear to those present at the meetings that action had to be taken against Levy. As a result an agreement was reached that Levy's 'Incredible' was to be boycotted from all DJ sets. Furthermore, any DJs, producers or promoters who were seen to be supporting Levy in any way would be similarly ostracised.

The situation created an immediate dilemma for the promoters. With their primary concern of getting punters through the door, Levy's chart status represented a guaranteed crowd-puller. He had subsequently been booked to play at venues throughout the country. At this late stage cancelling Levy's appearance would have resulted in the promoters getting sued for breach of contract. A move which would have bankrupted a number of organisations who had been hit by the falling numbers of ravers.

In full defiance of the committee, many clubs and raves decided to stay true to their obligations to General Levy. As a result of this the committee placed a full ban on anyone playing for these promoters. It was a decision which had an immediate impact on many DJs who depended on the rogue promoters for their living. One of those who stood most to lose was DJ Rap. Rap, ironically one of the few original DJs on the scene, declares:

All of that committee shit was a nightmare for me. I fell out with so many people who had been friends of mine. I thought the committee was set up to solve problems like pirate tapes and that, but it all turned into a big thing about a guy putting on a rave and us being told not to do it. Now I happen to have agreed with a lot of things that the committee said but if someone's booked me for five years, put money in my pocket for five years and then someone gets on the phone at four a.m. and says I can't play his raves any more it's not on. I'm loyal to the people who have booked me, it's my business. I'd have loved to have been involved with the committee if it had been run properly. I'm a part of this thing anyway but I'm not going to let someone tell me I can't do something just because they don't like the promoter.

With pressure mounting on General Levy, M Beat and Renk Records, the committee took the unprecedented step of pushing for a full letter of apology to be printed in *The Face*. It was the first time in history that representatives of a subculture had demanded the head of an individual, albeit in print. Levy eventually complied with the demand in the September 1994 issue of *The Face* and the committee began to realise how strong it could be. He wrote:

As a young, British, black artist I've had to struggle for years to get my break. I was DJing at Reggae dances when I was thirteen and have come up through the ranks of Reggae music so I know how hard it is to try and earn a living and make music you love. This makes me truly understand how much work the people in the Hardcore/Jungle community have had to put in for their music. Their love for what they do has enabled me to add a new dimension to my career. My quotes in your Jungle article (Face 71) failed to get this point across. I am part of a scene that is working to promote black music in this country. Anyone who wants to do the same I support and will big up. It is the DJs who supported Jungle (Randall, Micky Finn, Ray Keith, etc.), the shops (Blackmarket, Unity, etc.), the radio stations and the public who run Jungle. It is music by the people of the world. No one individual runs any type of music. I am but one voice trying to further the cause of black music in this country. General Levy, London.

However, the aims of the committee seemed to be far more than just concerned with a few Ragga MCs making a bit of money out of a scene with which they'd claimed an allegiance. The council was primarily made up of DJs and producers who had a vested interest in keeping the scene completely DJ led. With the Jungle sound being fronted by both the Ragga element and soulful vocalists like Elizabeth Troy (whose 'Greater Love' had recently gone into the national top twenty), the scene was starting to become artist based. And, as has already been pointed out, the promotion of the artist's personality represented the antithesis of the anonymity which the post-Acid House ravers had thrived on. Furthermore fully fledged Jungle artists brought the scene closer to the commercialised level of House. As a label which had invested in artists (ironically just as much as it had invested in producers and DJs) SOUR Records had a lot to lose. At the memory of the committee, Stone sighs:

The politics in this scene are worse than the Houses of Parliament. The council literally decided on whether people could or couldn't do things. They came down hard on the Ragga stuff and as a result the Ragga mix had had its day even before it peaked because of the politics. They were boycotting records everywhere. I had to fight tooth and nail to stop 'Original Nuttah' being boycotted and we'd done nothing wrong.

In the event 'Original Nuttah' became too popular among the crowds for any of the scene to ignore. However, the committee's desire to control things extended way beyond the Ragga crews. The Junglists' mistrust of all journalists had been compounded by the General Levy experience. By claiming that he'd been misquoted, he shifted the responsibility for his boasts on to the writer in question, thus pointing the finger at all journalists. As a result writers, film makers and anyone who could misrepresent the scene to the general public came under the scrutiny of the meetings. Once again Stone's SOUR Records was affected: 'They'd decide which journalists were OK to talk to,' he explains. 'If there was a documentary going on then they would decide who could get involved. I mean, we've got an eighteen-year-old artist with a top forty record and I'm being told *not* to do a BBC documentary. That was stupid.'

It's easy to get an image of the committee being little more than a group of people meeting in the smoky back room of a London pub, arguing over petty details which were of little concern to the future of the scene. Levy may have caused an uproar with his quotes and Ragga may have attempted to steal the increasingly tarnished Jungle crown, but the media had soon been put to rights on that issue. Indeed from this point on, many factions among the media have shown an almost paranoiac fear of representing the wrong people again, so proving that the meetings did have some positive effects. From here on, certain individuals were able to manipulate the media in order to present an at times almost rewritten account of what went on. If knowledge is indeed power then the Junglists were going to use their knowledge to control what was written about from now on.

In an interview on MTV's Partyzone Rebel MC hinted at the true intention of the committee. For him it was a necessary show of strength and a pooling of resources rather than a forum for petty arguments. 'I think first and foremost we have to deal with what we have now as a collective. We have to form a union, a foundation among ourselves. We have to build a foundation that's solid because before it goes anywhere else we have to take control so that it doesn't just get taken over by the industry, filter out and become just another little thing that came from England.'

Hindsight has shown how essential the committee actually was to the growth of the scene. More than just a platform for airing personal grievances, the coming together of Jungle's major players provided a chance to contemplate what could be done to avoid major labels from taking over just as they had with both Acid House and Hardcore. By this time many of the major players had been abused by major labels. Many others had simply been overlooked as not marketable enough. Subsequently many of the originators of Acid House, like A Guy Called Gerald, Jumping Jack Frost and Grooverider, had a real need to keep the future of Jungle under control. Indeed in many ways this Jungle collective could be seen as the underground rave scene growing up and facing the facts of business. The claim that Jungle was the sound of a more mature, adult Hardcore was one which has often been made. For DJ Rap the committee came to represent what was in many ways the end of Rave's youthful togetherness. The new unity was about the adult concerns of business. It was one of the basic principles of the commercial survival of what had, until now, been an entirely self sufficient guerilla industry. 'I think everyone was affected by the committee in some way. Basically it was the instant that I stopped raving. I just started thinking, "Fuck it, this is a business and that's the way I'm going to treat it",' says Rap of the changing climate in the scene and the altered attitudes of her contemporaries. This development had to happen for the scene to survive and conquer. It's a sentiment shared by Rob Playford who believes that what happened was merely a coming together of a number of people who'd been forced to learn about the business the hard way. 'What happened in 1994 was that business-wise and community-wise there were people who had been in it for three or four years then,' he argues. 'We'd all grown up a bit and we all knew each other so we all had a basic understanding of what we wanted. Which was basically a greater control over business and media.'

Naturally the Jungle industry, a group of individuals who had come to represent the very paradigm of underground culture, wanted to remain autonomous. However, with the increased popularity of the scene, both major and independent record labels had started to try and license tracks for compilations. The committee were apparently very wary of both the major labels and their compilations. After all hadn't labels like Ibiza's Jumpin' and Pumpin' been putting out superbly representative albums for ages now anyway?

In a move which echoed the situation with remixes, in-house studio engineers, always on the lookout for a way to earn extra money, saw the gap and started producing sub-standard tracks for compilations. The results may not have always been released but Dave Stone was particularly worried that the committee seemed to be doing little about this practice which he saw as being potentially damaging to the scene. 'The committee really presented simple choices of economics. They wanted to keep it underground, keep it real and at the same time people wanted to make a little bit of money out of it. Although they never seemed to confront the fact that they had to play the commercial game, to an extent they were setting themselves up for it,' explains Stone who had already started to take the SOUR DJs, producers and vocalists on tours to Japan and the USA in order to face up to the reality of Jungle's growing commercialisation. He continues:

The choice is you either get involved in the commercialisation of the scene or it becomes safe, although most people saw it as being the other way round. It's simple, if you're not going to put good tracks on to people's compilation albums, then someone in a little studio somewhere is going to see that there's some money to be made, knock two crap tracks together, license them and make all the money. That was proved by the rash of Jungle compilations which happened as every man and his dog jumped on the bandwagon in 1994. The only people who could stop them were the people who were making all this noise on the committee.

By the end of the year the secret meetings had fizzled out. Many found them to be a joke, soon realising that little was truly being achieved. However, if the committee had one positive point it forced what had largely been a disorganised group of people into taking stock of their own situation. For many it wasn't enough simply to play elitist games. They seriously wanted to push the music forward and the new found business strength afforded by the unity of the secret council encouraged many to take the major industry on.

Among these was Goldie who had long since been in meetings with major record labels. Not content with being well known in the rarefied circles of the scene, he wanted to take his crew to the next level and his vehicle was to be the astounding 'Timeless', a twenty-four-minute opus which brought forward a major label bidding war which London Records was ultimately to win.

However, in a move which was to be a testament to the concerns and ideals of both the Jungle scene and the committee, the deal was entirely on Goldie's terms, including total artistic control over choice of singles, cover artwork, videos, etc. and a compilation deal for his label Metalheads.

By achieving these aims Goldie and his associates not only succeeded in taking the Junglist cause overground but also managed to retain underground credibility. It was as if he'd scammed the major industry in a Drum 'n' Bass reworking of Robin Hood and in so doing remained true to his ideals, thus offering the truest representation of the committee's business aims.

It may have seemed like Jungle was really coming of age, but the truest indication of the future lay in the style which had almost universally been coined Drum 'n' Bass. A breakaway sound which was more melodic than the rough style of Jungle, Drum 'n' Bass showed a huge rift to have appeared in the scene, a split which resulted in two distinct camps. One side which was represented by the DJs who wanted to keep things raw, like the East End crew of De Underground, and the other side who aimed to take their more melodic sound towards both the club and the home listening audience, like L. T. J. Bukem.

7: INTELLIGENT MINDS OF JUNGLE

THE RISE OF AMBIENT DRUM 'N' BASS

I could knock out seventeen million Jungle tracks a week just by getting all my old Reggae seven inches and sticking them over an Amen break. I think people are more intelligent than that. I think people have got a lot more to offer.

L. T. J. Bukem

While the Jungle raves burned to the relentless sonic boom of Ragga another force was gently maturing behind closed studio doors. A smoother, more textural form of the Jungle equation which crossmatched spliced breaks with an ethereal ambience, cool Jazziness and soulful twists. The complete antithesis to the Jump Up sonics of the rugged and raw Junglist soundtrack, this new home listening version may have simply been referred to as Drum 'n' Bass by the artists involved, but promoters and journalists soon added the words Ambient or Intelligent to the description.

The implications of the 'Intelligent' tag had repercussions throughout the scene with Junglists complaining that it immediately implied that the Jump Up stuff was in some way stupid music for stupid people. Furthermore the term had racial implications since the Jungle raves were increasingly dominated by black youths, while this new strain of Drum 'n' Bass was allegedly aimed at a white audience.

Ironically Drum 'n' Bass was simply keeping the original ethos of Jungle alive. Concerned with pushing at the parameters of sound while employing influences from the entire spectrum of music, Drum 'n' Bass represented the very spirit of Jungle since its earliest House incarnations. Ragga-Jungle had become temporarily set in its ways, with carbon copy tracks being churned out by the dozen. Somehow the vitality in the music had gone, stifled by the demands of commercial success and instant gratification on the dancefloor.

The Drum 'n' Bass development of Breakbeat can, however, be seen taking place as far back as 1991. As T-Power has already suggested, Drum 'n' Bass and Jungle were developing side by side all along and, although very much in the minority, the more mellow style of Drum 'n' Bass was showing itself even during the Dark period.

One of the best known DJs exploring this development was L. T. J. Bukem. A pioneering DJ of the rave scene alongside Fabio and Grooverider, Bukem's musical tastes could be traced back to the jazzier happenings of Giles Peterson's Dingwalls sessions and even further to the Home Counties warehouse parties where Tim Westwood would spin selections of Hip Hop, Soul and Rare Groove. A long time sparring partner of Chalky Lom (Forces of Nature), Bukem was in every sense of the word a 1980s soulboy, his soundtrack for living provided by the Jazz Funk and Fusion sounds of Lonnie Liston Smith, Roy Ayers and Chic Corea. By the time Rave had hit he was DJing with a selection of Rare Groove, Jazz Funk and prime House tracks to a growing army of admirers.

Inevitably Bukem's first musical forays were going to represent his extremely varied tastes. His first, a simple mix 'n' match fusion of a Break-beat track and dub plate by New York House artists DeeLite, hardly lived up to Bukem's full promise. However, his follow up release 'Logical Progression', through Vinyl Mania in 1990 was, just as its title suggested, a shining beacon for a new direction.

By the time of his third release, he was living up to all expectations. Called 'Demon's Theme', it was both a huge leap forward in Breakbeat manipulation and an amazing statement of intent. Finished in early 1991 Bukem pressed up a dub plate to drop into his sets, not expecting any real reaction. However, quite unexpectedly 'Demon's Theme' caught people's imaginations immediately, its soulful combination of rushing breaks, lush ambience and mellow vibes opening up fresh vistas within the increasingly dark ambience of the rave. Among the apocalyptic clatter and machine gun vanities of Dark, where others would take the Breakbeat theme into the dense territories of Horrorcore psychosis and disturbed moodiness, Bukem introduced warmer vibes offering a rich pastoral oasis. He told *Muzik*'s Calvin Bush in 1995:

I called my first tune 'Logical Progression' because that's what it was. It was time for music to move on. I couldn't get the kind of music I wanted to play out, so I ended up making new tunes from finding beats and mixing them with House, and vice versa. It was the same when I made 'Demon's Theme' in 1992. The music was Dark then. Dark full stop. I'd been trying to get away from it, mixing it in with other stuff which was nicer.

A seemingly illogical digression from the contemporary scene, Bukem's opus had apparently painted him into a stylistic corner. His sets went increasingly against the grain with the Hardcore DJs joking about the soft nature of his mellow selections. Promoters chose to book him to play the four a.m. wind down sets and he looked like becoming known as one of Rave's mavericks, hidden away in the back rooms or lost in the twilight hours of the come down set.

Perhaps Bukem's biggest breakthrough came with his next release 'Music', which came out in 1993. For years he'd been using the Amen break within his sets, cutting and looping it in the Breakbeat tradition of Kool Herc. However, with 'Music' he finally converted it into the realms of his own personal musical vision. Solemn chords wove themselves around reverbed depth charges as a deep double bass line swung in a display of counter rhythmical interplay. The Amen break cut, spliced and contorted into a Funk fried monster. It proved to be a true landmark, with others soon taking the inspiration of 'Music' along their own paths. By early 1994 the queue of people joining forces with Bukem seemed endless.

Pete Parsons had engineered a series of stunning mellow and funky Drum 'n' Bass tunes for Dee Jay Recordings and Lucky Spin including 'One Line' by Fokus and DJ Crystal's 'Sweet Dreams'. Certificate 18 Records had started putting out dreamscaped Breakbeat collisions by artists as diverse as Sounds of Life (aka Source Direct) and Studio Pressure (aka Photek). Moving Shadow's Hardcore roots had now been completely displaced by the warmer vibes of Foul Play, Omni Trio and JMJ & Richie and even ruffneck Jungle imprints like La Bello Blanco started to push the tuneful vibes as pioneered by Bukem. Meanwhile the man's own label Good Looking was proving to be a dependable stable of sure shot talent with Peshay, Tayla and Wax Doctor turning in exhilarating performances on the early releases.

As Bukem's and his associate's own musical manoeuvres encompassed an ever wider spectrum, Ambient Drum 'n' Bass was being taken through an alternative series of breath taking sonic twists via Rob Haigh's releases under the alias of Omni Trio on Playford's Moving Shadow. A forceful combination of the rough edge of splintered beats and the smooth blanket of other-worldly Soul, Haigh's geographical situation alienated him from London's Dark vibes (he was based in East Anglia) giving him the space to turn the Hardcore sound through 360 degrees, bringing out a bliss-drenched liquid groove which took as much from the Industrial Funk scene of the 1980s (23 Skidoo, 400 Blows, Cabaret Voltaire, etc.) as it did from the positive soul of Rave. Released through Moving Shadow Records, 'Mystic Stepper (Feel Better)' and 'Renegade Snares' offered a perfect glimpse into a future filmesque sound of Jungle. 'We had Omni Trio in place at the exact time that the press really wanted to write about the right stuff,' argues Rob Playford of the universal acclaim that greeted Omni Trio. 'Rob Haigh fitted the bill perfectly for them. He was different from the rest of the stuff which was around and suddenly people got into it and realised that there was a history there.'

Perhaps the epitome of Breakbeat's 'eyes to the future' ideology and one of the scene's most influential labels is Reinforced Records. It was formed by West London Hardcore activists Mark Clair, Iain Bardouille, Gus Lawrence and Dego McFarlane. After coming together through their involvement with Camden based pirate station Long Island FM, the four-some started creating music as 4 Hero. Eventually they set up Reinforced out of the back of a record shop in the unlikely surroundings of the small Buckinghamshire town of Marlow-on-Thames.

From this point on, the label had always sought to release the best in underground House music. As such it has become an important barometer for future developments. Having initially explored the Hip House and then Hardcore scenes through their 4 Hero tracks, they went on to be influential figures in every subsequent development.

Already major players in the Dark period of late 1993, the label took the sound forward to the next level with its catalogue of seminal releases boasting a roll call of all of the scene's most creative and influential figures: Goldie (as Rufige Cru), L Double (who was previously with Sheffield's Unique 3), Lemon D, Stretch, Doc Scott and Grooverider. Together they created a selection of tunes which would range from the other-worldly Jazz contortions of Peshay's 'Protege' to the fractured breakscapes of Doc Scott's 'Last Action Hero'.

Reinforced's groundbreaking approach to music has resulted in them continually predicting the next sonic development in the Breakbeat science, displaying the future sound shifts which would continue to redefine the Drum 'n' Bass scene. Many of these changes could be heard on their essential series of EPs known as 'The Enforcers Series', each of which has consistently pointed to the possible ways forward, predicting each subsequent musical shedding.

By early 1994 however their eyes were set on a more Ambient style which would be as at home in clubs as it was on your personal stereo. Perhaps more abrasive than Bukem's watery grooves and certainly displaying more than a hint of a love for Hip Hop, the Reinforced version of ambient displayed a love of the Detroit Techno scene as much as the UK's Breakbeat renegades. Later that year Reinforced was to collect together some of the year's finer moments on a compilation called 'Intelligent Minds of Jungle'. A superbly unifying piece of plastic, it also displayed the scene's increased dissatisfaction with the term 'intelligent' which was still being used by the majority of commentators on Drum 'n' Bass. 'We were just trying to make a point', says Dego McFarlane. 'People were calling this stuff "intelligent" while the Jungle stuff was supposed to be unintelligent. We were just saying that all of this music comes from the intelligent minds of the Junglists and the whole history of House and Techno. Unfortunately people still didn't get it though!'

In June 1994 4 Hero (now reduced to the duo of Dego and Mark) released their debut album. Called 'Parallel Universe', it embraced the ideology of knowing no boundaries, seeping the Breakbeats into the cracks of any music they wanted to appropriate. A landmark album, 'Parallel Universe' wandered through experimental Jazz terrain, drawing on b-boy roots whilst layering the crystal clear breaks with washes of lush strings.

Writing about the album some two years later Tim Barr described it as 'A triumph of Breakbeat science . . . From the supernova lovers' rock of "Universal Love" to the compelling percussive ballet of "Solar Emissions", this is the record which took Drum 'n' Bass into outer space.' Indeed he goes on to sum up 'Parallel Universe' as 'A piece of musical futurism that's still deeply, absurdly essential'.

Justified praise indeed as 'Parallel Universe' not only opened the doors for the artist-led Drum 'n' Bass album in the long run, but it also pointed directly to the scene's ongoing fascination for Jazz. It provided a new term with which to collect together the musical Drum 'n' Bass artists.

JAZZ STEP

By the close of 1994 is was the Jazzier landscape that had caught the Drum 'n' Bass fraternity's imagination. It's of little surprise that the scene should have taken this route. The increasingly complex Breakbeat structures were sounding similar to the Jazz Fusion rhythms of bands like Weather Report, while this genre of musicians was also proving to be an important source of raw material to sample.

Bukem's influence had brought people into the Breakbeat scene who would normally have rejected it out of hand – the Jazz and Rare Groove pundits associated with Acid Jazz and Talkin' Loud, the Giles Peterson crowd. With them came a fresh set of influences and an in depth knowledge of Jazz. Meanwhile Reinforced's adoption of a Jazzier vibe immediately excited the inner sanctum of the Drum 'n' Bass scene with Fabio taking every opportunity to mesh Jazzy stuff with his Breakbeat sets.

The final piece in the Jazzy Drum 'n' Bass jigsaw came as the influence of Detroit Techno started to surface. Originally inspired by the electronic music of German band Kraftwerk, the Detroit artists gradually fused the cold certainty of Techno with the spiritually uplifting warmth of Jazz. In a move echoed by the Junglists a number of years later, Detroit Techno became a crossroads where tight rhythmical intricacy would meet lush string motifs and counter melodic refrains. In 1994 the Detroit Techno scene was being eulogised by the UK's dance industry and by early 1995 it ruled both the club circuit and the pages of the specialist magazines as people became fascinated with a search for musical authenticity in times of cultural uncertainty.

With the onset of 1995 the Jazz element within the Ambient Drum 'n' Bass sound started to come to the fore. Among the breakthrough tracks to reference this fascination with Jazz was 'Jazz Note' by Bristol's DJ Krust on Brian Gee's V Recordings. A huge club favourite with its off beat electric piano motif, sweeping strings and rolling beats 'Jazz Note' offered a slice of pure class which set a new standard among the Drum 'n' Bass fraternity.

While Bristol's DJ Krust and partner Roni Size set off down their own unique path which would find them stripping the sound down to its simplest, yet most challenging Jazz Step form, the Home Counties area of Marlow, High Wycombe and Reading was growing as the centre of a Jazzy Drum 'n' Bass sound which was closer to the vibes coming from the Bukem camp. If this development had already been pioneered by north west London's Good Looking Records, then an arsenal of supporting labels soon developed with Reading's Vinyl Distribution acting as a connecting point for everyone. The distribution company's own Precious Materials and Basement Records paving the way with some excellent releases from Wax Doctor, Alex Reece and Luton's Blame and Justice.

As Reading started to be seen as the business centre for Jazzy Drum 'n' Bass, the creative epicentre had emerged in High Wycombe. Known as the heartland of the soulboy in the early 1980s, High Wycombe and its surrounding area seemed to be imbued with a Jazz Funk ambience which seeped into a number of its local producers' sound banks. Among the artists to pick up on this vibe and then translate it into the realms of Drum 'n' Bass were Wax Doctor (from Marlow), DJ Pulse and Stretch. Together they formed Creative Wax, one of the scene's premier labels.

Among the first artists to release tracks through Creative Wax was Ealing's Alex Reece whose name was, in the media's view, soon to become synonymous with the Jazz sound. Reece initially came to music through his involvement with Jack Smooth (later releasing dreamscaped Drum 'n' Bass as Mystic Moods) on a project called Electronic Experience. It was a brooding mixture of Dark strings, heavy Techno and a beat which married the four to the floor bass drum with the funked up Breakbeat. Working as an engineer for Basement Records he twiddled knobs for legendary Hardcore DJs like Loftgroover before eventually setting up his own bedroom studio called the Acid Lab.

The studio freedom this provided resulted in singles for Labworks and Sinister but it was only after he collaborated with Wax Doctor and DJ Pulse that he fully opened up to Drum 'n' Bass's potential. Together the three-some produced a series of deeply funky club floor tracks under the aliases of Unit 1, Fallen Angels and Radioactive Kids.

It soon became obvious that Reece had a keen love and understanding for the Detroit Techno sound. His tracks were increasingly reminiscent of artists like Larry Heard and Derrick May and by the time he released the superb 'Detroit' under the name 'Jazz Juice', his status was secured. Up until this point he was seen very much as a part of a threesome with Pulse and Wax.

In early 1994, however, Reece created his first solo cut 'Basic Principles', which Fabio immediately previewed on dub plate. It soon came to the ears of Goldie who himself was in the throws of setting up a new label. Later that year 'Basic Principles' came out on Goldie's Metalheads imprint, instantly creating a buzz among the Drum 'n' Bass fraternity. The follow up, 'B-boys Flavour', may not have been so well received but the 1995 release of 'Pulp Fiction' went way beyond all expectations. Soon becoming a soundtrack to the scene it was voted single of the year in the 1995 Hardcore awards while also receiving accolades beyond the call of duty in the press. A stunning tune, it married a simple break with a haunting horn refrain, both light and dark at the same time, the wash of disconnected ambience offering the tune a sinister underbelly. 'Pulp Fiction' caught the ears of the major record industry and the inevitable bidding war emerged with Reece eventually signing to Island, who had soon realised the commercial potential in the Jazz Drum 'n' Bass sound.

In an attempt to define this musical form Simon Reynolds coined the term 'Artcore'. Drawing immediate allusions to the Ambient Drum 'n' Bass fraternity's often documented love of the soundtrack, it also highlighted the attitude of musical superiority which was being placed upon this music. An attitude which was encompassed by 'Hardcore's shift towards a self-conscious "maturity",' as Simon Reynolds put it. Drawing attention to the extent to which Jungle and Drum 'n' Bass had become divided Reynolds also noted that 'some of Jungle's experimental vanguard resort to the same rhetoric once used – by evangelists for Progressive House or Techno – to dismiss Hardcore as "juvenile" and "anti-musical". Usually,' he continues, 'this progressive discourse masks a class-based or generational struggle to seize control of music's future.'

Remarks which incensed the purveyors of Drum 'n' Bass who still regarded their roots as firmly within the underground culture of Rave. If, as Reynolds seemed to be suggesting, Drum 'n' Bass was the sound of the middle classes going through a process of gaining control of the Breakbeat scene then it would go hand in hand with the dealings of the committee which had aimed to run Jungle from the inside. It could be said that the Drum 'n' Bass scene took the same ideals of control as preached by the infamous committee and used them for their own ends, turning Drum 'n' Bass into the dominant form of Breakbeat.

Indeed as 1995 progressed the melodic Drum 'n' Bass style was increasingly championed by the media. It was a style which journalists could happily listen to without ever going to a rave: a seemingly upwardly mobile style which fitted easily into the value systems of musicality and authenticity which have always dominated music criticism. Furthermore, Drum 'n' Bass came pre-packaged with its own figureheads like Goldie and Bukem who were even prepared to criticise the Ragga-Jungle sound. Indeed the journalistic notion of Artcore seemed to embrace all of the concerns of the middle classes. As such the Ambient Drum 'n' Bass form from which Artcore was derived was increasingly referred to as white music, whilst Ragga-Jungle came to be seen as a black domain. Whether or not this was true, the roots of Jungle were becoming increasingly blurred.

SPEED

For the fans of Ambient Drum 'n' Bass, the only way that this new sound could be enjoyed from late 1993 and for much of 1994 was via the experimental shows on pirate stations. It was a difficult time when Ragga-Jungle ruled the clubbing roost and although Bukem and Fabio played the style at some of the raves, there was nowhere that could be called the home of Drum 'n' Bass.

In October 1994 all of this changed. Fabio, Bukem, Kemistry and Storm and a selection of guests took over the Mars Bar in London's West

End for a Monday night session. Called Speed, the night was to become one of the country's most important club nights. Indeed, as a creative centre for Drum 'n' Bass its importance was paramount. A meeting place for like-minded producers, DJs and punters, it was a million miles from the Jungle raves which were raging to crowds upwards of 5000 in other parts of the country. With a capacity of only a few hundred, Speed was the every epi-centre of this growing scene and in many ways the catalyst which Ambient Drum 'n' Bass had needed.

But Speed wasn't always a force to be reckoned with, its opening night only drew a small handful of people to enjoy the vibes. The second and third weeks were no better with the door tax hardly being enough to cover costs. With a lot of suspicion coming from the Hardcore Breakbeat fans who considered that Speed's status as a West End club was selling out the underground, it looked as though Speed was going to remain the Drum 'n' Bass scene's best kept and shortest lived secret as the same faces came each week, sitting around the edges of the dancefloor, smoking weed and watching the few people brave enough to dance. 'I remember going on the opening night and it seemed empty,' reminisces Zoe Richardson who went on to co-promote PM Scientists while also DJing and promoting Drum 'n' Bass. 'I was totally blown away by so much wicked music I'd never heard before, and I'd been into it since the early days. It was amazing.'

With the promoters considering shutting the doors once and for all if things didn't improve, they tried changing nights to a Thursday and sud-denly the unexpected happened. With no apparent reason other than word of mouth and a general increased interest in Drum 'n' Bass, the fifth week of Speed found the queue stretching down the road and round the corner of Soho Square. People were buzzing, totally amazed that the club had been going so long without them knowing. These weren't people who had just discovered the sound, it transpired. These were the people who hadn't been a part of the A.W.O.L. clique but had tuned into Drum 'n' Bass through the pirate stations. A whole new generation of Breakbeat freaks, Junglists and Drum 'n' Bass heads searching for their own Paradise. Indeed Speed was to Drum 'n' Bass what Roast had been to Jungle and Rage to Hardcore.

The Mars Bar was a darkened basement with a dingy ambience, yet Speed managed to transform it into a Utopia of sub bass frenzy. A sweatbox where the people were cooler than the drinks in the cabinet, Speed saw the clothing style move away from the flesh-revealing Lycra and the designer casual chic. In its place came a fashion more in line with a Hip Hop tradition. Nikes sat with Tommy Hilfiger as the street style of the Bronx merged with London suss. The drugs too had all but disappeared with weed and champagne being the order of the day.

Each week Fabio and Bukem would ply their smooth and rolling breaks. Bukem on the oceanic tip, washing the crowd with lush string drive epics while Fabio took the vibe deeper into Jazz land. Intricate beats intertwined with strolling bass lines, counter tempos and off key refrains. Meanwhile Kemistry and Storm cooked up a different brew with a glimpse into the chemistry labs of the country's sonic scientists, revealing strangeness and wonder from the likes of Source Direct and Photek.

It was an exhilarating mix of DJs all pointing towards possible futures, each as interesting as the other and inevitably after three months the word had spread to the ears of the media and the music industry. It was 1995, Goldie's 'Inner City Life' had been released to universal acclaim and everyone was sniffing around for a slice of the Drum 'n' Bass pie. Suddenly the euphoric energy of this dingy basement club transformed into a meet and greet of the industry sharks. It was a sea of networking PR types, media babes looking for the in place, foreign TV crews and of course A&R men looking for new remixers, waving chequebooks under the noses of every DJ they managed to talk to. If ever the industry overkill had been evident it was at Speed.

Happily the hype soon died down and the weekenders, fair-weather Junglists and story-mongering journos fled the scene in search of fresh carrion. The club continued as the central venue it had originally been but the spirit seemed slightly drained. The lifeblood of Speed had been sucked by the needs and greeds of the major industry and the club no longer walked with the same arrogant pride as before. By the summer of 1995 the weekly turnout was returning to the trickle of its earliest nights and in early 1996 L. T. J. Bukem announced that he was leaving among rumours of arguments between him and Fabio.

It was the end of another era for the Breakbeat, but in typical style it only heralded the start of the next stage.

RECOMMENDED LISTENING

'The Angels Fall' – Dillinja (Metalheads)

'Music' – L. T. J. Bukem (Looking Good)

'On Line' – Focus (Dee Jay Recordings)

'Exit 9' – Source Direct (Source Direct)

'One and Only' – PFM (Good Looking)

'The Western' – PFM (Good Looking)

'Horizons' – L. T. J. Bukem (Good Looking)

'Aromatherapy' – Adam F (Section 5)

'Drift to the Centre' – Aquarius (Looking Good)

'Atmospheric Funk' – Wax Doctor (Talkin' Loud)

'The Water Margin' – Photek (Photek)

'Pulp Fiction' – Alex Reece (Metalheads)

'Mutant Jazz' – T Power V. MK Ultra (SOUR)

'Taken Over' – Fallen Angels (Creative Wax)

'Nine Lives' – Underwolves (Filter)

'Psychosis' – Peshay (Metalheads)

'Circles' – Adam F (Sector 5)

'Renegade Snares' – Omni Trio (Moving Shadow)

'Wrinkles in Time' – 4 Hero (Reinforced)

'Dolphin Tune' – Aquarius (Good Looking)

'A Made Up Sound' – Source Direct (Metalheads)

'Is it Love' – Hidden Agenda (Metalheads)

8: FEEL THE SUNSHINE

TAKING ON THE MAINSTREAM

As the smoother sonics of Bukem, Reece and their ilk dominated the Summer of 1995 other artists took the Jazz on a much darker route. Sourcing the head spinning intensity of artists like Miles Davis and concentrating their full on euphoria into the actual rhythmic structure, a darker, perhaps more demanding unnamed form of Drum 'n' Bass emerged, although like all of the various strands within the Jungle fabric, its roots can be traced back to Dark.

It was a musical transformation which seemed to bear little relation to its Hardcore roots beyond the source material of the Breakbeat. Displaying a high degree of musical ability coupled with extreme programming skill, this Drum 'n' Bass development saw an even more intense coming together of opposites (rough with smooth, up front energy with laid back vibes).

However, if any track had previously hinted at this technologically progressive direction it was Goldie's astonishing marriage of deconstructed breaks and aching Soul which could be found on his 1994 single 'Angel'. Combining samples lifted from David Byrne and Brian Eno's seminal 'My Life in the Bush of Ghosts' which were then poured into a mélange of splintered metallic beats and Diane Charlemagne's surreal Soul croon, 'Angel' was the meeting place between the desperate nihilism of Dark and the brave new world ethos of experimental Drum 'n' Bass. Ambient in the sense that it used textual flourishes of strings, yet somehow foreboding, it is drenched in a feeling of fear which drags you down in an exhilarating battle of passions; life versus death, good against evil, poverty versus wealth. 'Rufige was the way you described things just lying around on the surface – more or less scum – which you collected together and turned into something new,' Goldie explains. 'I was using fourth and fifth generation samples, just trash sounds, but they had the grittiness and roughness which identified with the feel of the street.'

However, Goldie felt that he hadn't come close to exploring technology's true potential. Hooking up for days at a time with Mark and Dego of Reinforced he would push equipment, ideas and imagination to the very limits in a quest for that groundbreaking ambience. Talking to Tim Barr in 1996 Goldie recalls:

I remember one session which we did which lasted for over three days . . . just experimenting, pushing the technology to its limits. We'd come up with mad ideas and then try to recreate them. We filled tape after tape with this stuff. We were sampling ourselves, and then re-sampling, twisting sounds around and pushing them into all sorts of places – and I think we kinda wrote the manual over those three days.

Indeed it was a collection of ideas inspired by the writing of this manual which Goldie took in the shape of DATs and samples to Rob Playford's studio in Hertfordshire.

Although 'Inner City Life' failed to live up fully to its commercial potential, failing even to dent the national top forty, it did promise that the forthcoming album would be breathtaking. With many of the album's tracks a permanent feature at Speed, the clues were already there for people to pick up on. When it was finally released in October 1995, however, the response was overwhelming. One of the most inspired albums of the last thirty years, 'Timeless' was a heart-stopping monster which contained more ideas in each track than most would come up with on an entire album. Reviewing the album at the time *Melody Maker*'s David Stubbs said:

It isn't just on a purely visceral level; 'Timeless' is a relentlessly awesome compendium of the hardest, fastest, most pulse-racing, shocking, inventive,

most sophisticated and finely wrought modernistic music you'll hear
anywhere right now, as state of the art as 'Terminator V'. This is more than
just a sonic slalom through some of Jungle's darkest, outermost and
undiscovered thickets. This is like the man boasts. This is art.

'Timeless' represented the first real crossover into the mainstream of
any of the Jungle/Drum 'n' Bass tracks and as such it remains a landmark
release. What is also interesting is the fact that Goldie managed to adhere
to major label marketing restrictions, court the media (with many referring
to him as 'Jungle's first star') and flaunt his new found prosperity while still
being regarded from within the scene as a representative of the underground.

The simple fact of the matter was that although Goldie may have
moved into the major league, he hadn't lost any of his musical integrity. He
remained the b-boy personified. Although he did go to extreme lengths to
point out that he was an artist (with a graffiti bombing past) who had a
vision beyond the here and now of club culture. 'In there ["Timeless"] is
everything I've learned from music, everyone I've met, everything I've
experienced,' he argues, elevating the album beyond the street level
demands of dance music and into the realms of the street cool auto-
biography. It's a story about his life, his surroundings and his own particular take on life – a concept for the Breakbeat scientists – 'Timeless'.

THE ARTIST ALBUM

Both Jungle and Drum 'n' Bass were extensively promoted via the compilation album. For each new variation on the theme came a new collection;
each label presented its own long playing round-up. Even promoters like
Desert Storm and A.W.O.L. put out their mix sets. The compilations offered
the best way for people to discover the scene without having to shell out a
fortune for singles. Furthermore the rest of the UK wasn't as well serviced
with records as London, so these underground selections became essential
for the proliferation of the scene.

As the DJs' role as the artist grew in stature, so too did their needs to
put out full length albums. And, given the home listening nature of much of
Drum 'n' Bass, it was these artists who first tapped into the album market.

Goldie's 'Timeless' may well have proved to be the scene's most successful album to date, thanks not only to the music it contained but also to the huge marketing campaign. However the first Drum 'n' Bass artist album was 4 Hero's 'Parallel Universe', although it's interesting to note that this record was soon 'lost', due to the meagre finances available because of its independent status.

The funds needed to keep a dance related album in the public's consciousness was a critical factor in the lack of long term success for a number of Breakbeat artist albums during 1995. Perhaps the most infamous of these was A Guy Called Gerald's 'Black Secret Technology' on his own Juicebox Records which came out in the spring of that year. Despite rave reviews in the national press and a fantastic response from the Drum 'n' Bass underground, it disappeared from the stockists' shelves soon after release.

In many ways the stylistic forerunner to Goldie's 'Timeless' (Goldie and Gerald collaborated on one track, 'Energy'), 'Black Secret Technology' tapped into the black science fiction tradition drawing a line from Sun Ra through to Doc Scott, taking in technological experimentalists Derrick May and Afrika Bambaataa along the way. Sweeping the spectrum of black technology influenced music from Detroit Techno to Electro, dub Reggae to Hip Hop, Gerald succeeded in creating a collection of tracks which sound both urgent and, yes, timeless.

The production of 'Black Secret Technology' may have been stunning, a mind boggling array of cut ups, backward reverbs, sub bass and filtering, but Gerald never lost sight of the primal energy of the Breakbeat. Keeping the atmosphere physically centred yet spiritually uplifting, never did 'Black Secret Technology' turn into an indulgent mess of head music. Indeed it remains one of the most complete sounding Drum 'n' Bass albums to date. Two years later in January 1997, Gerald released a new version of 'Black Secret Technology' complete with extra tracks and a couple of remixes. As a testament to Gerald's genius it still sounded as fresh on its second release.

Although the so-called Ambient/Intelligent axis has become the area most associated with the artist album, two of the earliest full length efforts were from artists more closely associated with Jungle. Bristol's 'More Rockers', aka Rob Smith and Peter D, circulated white labels of their 'Dub Plate Selection Volume 1' as early as November 1994 although it didn't see a final release until the spring of 1995. An awesome selection, it drew on every aspect of the black musical form, showing a huge debt to the Reggae soundsystem along the way. Quite at odds with the Techno influenced sounds of the Jazz-Junglists and Ambient Drum 'n' Bass heads, More Rockers employed live sounding drum breaks to construct a sound which moved between soulful vocal performances and samples of Jamaican Reggae giants like Frankie Paul and Johnny Osborne. Unlike the Ragga-Junglist sound which found much of its style in 1980s soundsystem developments, this album found its foundation deep in the smoke filled vibes of 1970s Reggae.

Also steeped in a Reggae tradition was 'Champion Jungle Sound' by the Kemet Crew, which echoed the contemporary Ragga and vocal developments in Jungle. Released in the summer of 1995 on the RCA subsidiary Parousia, 'Champion Jungle Sound' comprised a collection of Mark X produced tracks typifying the ruffneck breaks that Kool FM were airing every night. Although displaying incredible Breakbeat dexterity the album didn't have the depth needed to sustain a longplayer, while it also suffered at the hands of a media who were more interested in the Ambient Drum 'n' Bass scene. For Mark X, however, the aims of the album weren't simply to represent the word of Jungle but also as a vehicle for his Muslim faith.

Later that year SOUR Records jumped head first into the artists' market with releases from Shy FX and T-Power. Exploring the styles presented in his 'Gangsta Kid' and 'Original Nuttah' singles, Shy FX's 'Just an Example' was a disappointing selection of Jump Up versions offering nothing new to the story. T-Power's debut album was another story.

Called 'Self Evident Truth of an Intuitive Mind' it sidestepped the popularity of T-Power and MK Ultra's classic and much licensed Jazzy Jungle track 'Mutant Jazz' and went straight for the jugular with dense experimental beats. Although flawed due to the occasionally static beats, it was a collection which showed the vast areas open to the individual who was prepared to take this sound away from the popular view of Drum 'n' Bass. Where Bukem and friends were creating inviting oceanic sounds, T-Power offered a foreboding dissonance, a bleak isolationist vision of a world under the intruding eye of surveillance cameras. If there was a sound of the concrete Jungle facing up to the reality of life in the 1990s then it surely could be found on this album.

Hotly tipped as being the artist most likely to follow in Goldie's foot-steps was Alex Reece. His debut album came out via major label Island Records with a massive push behind it. Reece had already won over a huge number of people outside the scene with his 'Pulp Fiction' single on Metalheads. His first single for the new company, however, managed even better things. Initially released towards the end of 1995 'Feel the Sunshine' disappeared under the weight of the Christmas rush. But with its re-release three months later the ultra smooth Björkesque Jazz Funk Drum 'n' Bass workout became the scene's first top forty hit of 1996.

Naturally Reece's album was one of the most eagerly awaited since Goldie's, but when pre-tapes started circulating, murmurs of disappoint-ment could be heard everywhere. With its subsequent release you could hardly hear the track for the sound of the Drum 'n' Bass scene turning their backs on last year's hero. Although it was given favourable reviews in the press, 'those that know' were quick to dismiss it.

Sounding at times almost incomplete, 'So Far' showed Alex Reece to be someone who perhaps wasn't quite ready to release an album. His tunes had always been aimed at the dancefloor and as such lacked the depth needed to sustain a full length album. In many ways it came as a warning to the rest of the scene who had been talking about albums at the time. The transition wasn't an easy one as Reece had shown, so the other artists who had by this time been signed to majors, Roni Size to Talking Loud, Photek and Source Direct to Virgin, Grooverider to Sony, Peshay to Mo'Wax, etc., wisely opted to take their time over the process.

DRUM 'N' BASS GOES LIVE

A less appealing side of this belief in the creative superiority of experi-mentalism was an increased movement towards the kind of muso snob-bery which had dogged the world of rock in the years prior to Punk. If Jungle's Jump Up energy was the electra-sonic equivalent of the Clash or the Sex Pistols, then so-called Artcore was potentially the new Progressive Rock!

Increasingly seated in the realms of coffee table listening the Ambient/Intelligent scene moved away from its Hardcore roots. The artists, however, needed to find a way of placing their music out of the studios and back into the public domain – by going out live.

For artists like Shy FX and DJ SS the live experience was nothing new. They'd been a regular PA feature at the Jungle raves for a couple of years. For Goldie, however, the live show represented a mammoth but necessary task, if his album was to cross over into the consciousness of the wider public. Playing live was essential, as the best selling dance acts like Orbital, Underworld, Leftfield and the Chemical Brothers had all proved. Goldie, keen to take his message to as many people as possible, set about putting together a band.

In fact it turned out to be more of a travelling Metalheadz package as the label's artists acted as DJs before and after the band and the entire show was MCd by Cleveland Watkiss, who also made a guest appearance on the slow jam 'Sea of Tears'. Goldie's band featured both himself and Rob Playford manipulating the racks of samplers and effects while out front Lorna Harris took the vocal role.

The 'Goldie Presents Metalheads' show debuted in America in late 1995 but it wasn't until March 1996 that it touched down on the crew's home soil of London. Anticipation was at a massive high as queues snaked around the Forum in Kentish Town, London, touts selling tickets at four times their face value. In the event, however, the Metalheads Show was poorly received, much of the crowd either too new to the sound to cope with its peaks and troughs, older converts simply hungry for the Hardstep and Rollers sets of the DJs like Randall, Grooverider and Doc Scott. People simply became bored by Goldie's elongated Ambient passages, the performance itself lacking the dynamic urgency that Breakbeat had always sparked. Reviewing the gig in *Melody Maker*, I was hardly able to hide my disappointment, a sentiment shared by so many others. I wrote:

Forty-five minutes in and something's got to give. 'This one's for the people who said we couldn't make real music', states Goldie introducing the Jazz Funk opus 'State of Mind'. Where the album cut is a smoking cauldron of seductive vibes, the live version stumbles into overblown muso territory, an Eighties ambience bringing the atmosphere way down. 'You & Me' and 'A Sense of Rage' both try to work their magic but the spell has been broken.

Where the show may have disappointed a hard-to-please home audience, it was abroad where things really worked. Touring with Icelandic avant garde pop singer Björk across America the sound of Drum 'n' Bass, Goldie-style, reached a whole new set of converts. The same was true across Europe where Goldie's evocative style captured the imaginations of people who had probably never even heard of Jungle before. In the end the tour was a resounding success, helping to push sales of 'Timeless' to 100,000 in the UK alone, while also taking the word of Drum 'n' Bass to its widest audience yet.

And by the time the show returned to England at the end of the summer for Universe's 'Big Love' festival, the Goldie revue had tightened up so much that the performance had been transformed into a stunning marriage of Motown Funk and urban flash. If Jungle's earliest incarnation had been the sound of joyriders ram-raiding the window fronts of the establishment, then Goldie live had become the soundtrack to cruising around town in your Mercedes Benz, flashing your gold-plated wheel hubs.

With Goldie's success the move towards the live arena seemed almost inevitable. Artists as diverse as Voyager, DJ Rap and T-Power geared up to take their Drum 'n' Bass visions into the gig arena.

In 1996, acclaimed Jazz Junglist Adam F played his first live dates to promote his 'F-Jam' single. A track which featured a full complement of live musicians along with the vocal talent of MC Conrad, it sparked two distinctly different reactions. On the one hand his obvious accomplishment as a musician brought admiration from the musical side of the Drum 'n' Bass scene. Indeed a dub plate of 'F-Jam' became a regular in the sets of Fabio and Bukem (along with newcomers PM Scientists) for months prior to its release (and subsequent re-release on major Positiva), its classic status almost undisputed among the mellower Drum 'n' Bass fraternity. On the other hand, however, Adam F's overwhelming musical ability brought condemnation from others. Considering Adam F's muso approach (he was once a session musician for the Moody Blues), some feared that this was simply a vindication of Simon Reynolds's claims two years earlier that Drum 'n' Bass was the sound of the middle classes, too wrapped up in the musician's hierarchy of skill over content. This attitude gave Drum 'n' Bass an overwhelming sense of superiority over its non-musical roots in Hardcore and Jungle.

In an interview with Adam F in *Mixmag*, Bethan Cole notes: '. . . there's a dangerous complacency among producers like Adam F that their music is more intellectually advanced, sophisticated and mature than anyone else's.'

If the live domain is where these same producers aimed to show their sophistication and maturity, Omni Trio's Rob Haigh expressed his concerns about it as much as three years earlier:

House and Jungle are sequenced music, created on computer workstations. We are not ashamed of that. There's nothing worse than seeing House musicians trying to get into that live music vibe. The live element of our music occurs on the dancefloor. There's unlimited potential for the atmospheric, multitextured, intelligent direction in Hardcore, but it must retain the roughness of a tearing Drum 'n' Bass base. To lose it would be like Rock music without guitars.

Drum 'n' Bass may have gone live, but to what expense?

ONE IN THE JUNGLE

The growing popularity of Jungle and its Drum 'n' Bass counterpart both here and abroad could no longer be ignored by the UK's national popular music station, Radio One. Although a long time feature of John Peel's eclectic show, the BBC's powers that be had decided to make a real commitment to dance culture and black music. Among the new proposals was a show called 'One in the Jungle' which was to be a series tracing the history of the scene over a seven-week period. OK, so not exactly a long term commitment, but a change all the same.

'One in the Jungle' was the brainchild of Brian Belle-Fortune, a regular face on the Jungle scene since his move to London a couple of years earlier. Through his passion for Jungle he'd developed a close association with Kool FM and many of the DJs, so when the concept of a Radio One Jungle show came up in conversation he was quick to act.

With a rough proposal he met with the bosses of Radio One as early as 1994. They employed him immediately, asking him to set about putting the show together. Drawing on some of the scene's best known names like Brockie, Jumping Jack Frost and Hype he put together a show which not only satisfied the listener used to the roughness of the pirates but also met with the commercial concerns of the BBC. On 27 July 1995 the first show in the series was transmitted to huge acclaim. And then, with the series finished – silence.

In March 1996, however, Aunty Beeb announced that their cob-webbed corridors were to be opened up to a regular slot for the 'One in the Jungle' show from April onwards. Ironically the announcement came at a time when every independent station in the land was showing a vote of 'no confidence' and axing its specialist Jungle shows. For example, Galaxy Radio in Bristol had recently ditched their hugely popular 'Full Circle Show' with DJ Krust and Roni Size, a move which said more about the narrow-minded programming adopted by regional radio than any loss of popular-ity of the actual music.

On the face of it Radio One's decision would seem to be unpreced-ented. However, a closer look suggested the BBC were simply systemat-ically stealing Kiss FM's best ideas and most experienced personnel in an effort to gain underground credibility. Indeed in a controversial move the BBC decided not to use Belle-Fortune as producer for the new series, and took on board the man responsible for Kiss's own Jungle shows, Wilber Wilberforce. 'The main problem was that I was pretty inexperienced and I just watched people taking my best ideas,' complained Belle-Fortune a couple of weeks before the new series went out on air. 'I mean, I got on really well with Andy Parfitt (managing editor) because he was genuinely interested on a street level. So he was totally into my plans for the series. Unfortunately other people weren't so receptive. I would say that there was a total poverty of ideas at Radio One at that time.'

A number of people within the Jungle community were unhappy about Radio One's involvement. To them it was no different to the General Levy fiasco when the media had no idea what it was doing. They should have left it to Kiss and Kool to represent. Leave things to 'those that know'. Radio One was just a bandwagon-jumping corporate who didn't have an original idea in its head – stealing ideas from London's infinitely more popular (among the dance audience) Kiss FM. 'It's not really a question of whether

Kiss had the ideas first,' argues Wilberforce. 'Radio One is a much bigger concern and as such the wheels turn more slowly than at a smaller station like Kiss. The BBC can't respond immediately to underground scenes but they do have a commitment to give the public what they want. After all it's the public who pay the wages.'

What the public seemed to want of course was Jungle. The Jungle scene, however, still had its doubts and thought that the BBC team would get the wrong people to represent Jungle. Ironically it was Wilberforce himself who had created perhaps the biggest problem here. In his days at Kiss he'd got the DJs to sign exclusivity contracts so he was unable to use the bigger names like Fabio, Grooverider and Bukem. In the end, he was able to put together a stunning array of DJs representing the whole spectrum of the Jungle/Drum 'n' Bass scene. DJs like Size and Krust, Kenny Ken, Mickey Finn and Nicky Blackmarket – many of the mainstays of Kool FM in fact. 'The good thing is that we haven't had to concentrate on the chosen few,' Wilberforce explains. 'There are too many good DJs around and we want to be a forum for these people as well as the better known names. In the end this show will grow with Jungle and continue to represent it as accurately as possible.'

Indeed the ratings and popularity of 'One in the Jungle' had proven that this sound could be as popular across the entire country as it was in London. In effect the BBC had joined MTV in opening up the Jungle and Drum 'n' Bass phenomenon to the rest of the country.

UK GROWTH OF THE SCENE

Since the sound of Dark first emerged in the early 1990s there had always been pockets of Breakbeat devotees throughout the country. Areas like the Hardcore stronghold of the Midlands, where Doc Scott pushed the Coventry vibes and DJ SS who bigged up Leicester. Similarly the south coast had long been a Hardcore zone which made an early transition towards Jungle.

Perhaps the most important area outside London has been Bristol. Home of the slow beats of Trip Hop, Bristol has also pioneered the Jazz Step sound via artists like Roni Size, DJ Krust, Suv and Die through their Full Cycle label. Also prominent have been Flyn and Flora who record for and own the Independent Dealers imprint while the More Rockers Collective output has included albums by Henry and Louis called 'Rudiments', the hugely influential Smith and Mighty with 'Bass is Maternal' and Smith's other project 'More Rockers'.

If there is a Bristol sound then it is typified by what Phil Johnson describes in his book *Straight Outta Bristol* as '. . . echoing the Reggae roots and Trip Hop slackness of the earlier Bristol Hip Hop producers'. Indeed there seems to be a laid back spirit running through the Bristol scene: even at its most Hardstep or Jump Up the vibrant urgency of the skidding breaks is countered by a supine ambience which brings to mind the smoky ambience of a Reggae blues party or the subsonic boom of a Reggae sound-system in full flow.

With the popularity of the sound came the inevitable Jungle events in the shape of 'Ruffneck Ting', run by the Colin Stevens and the *Knowledge* fanzine team. A regular event featuring resident sets from local DJ Dazee, Ruffneck Ting lived up to its name with nights of pure Jump Up. Regular guests included premier league DJs with Micky Finn, Bryan Gee, Randall, Kenny Ken, Hype and Rap being among the most popular.

Despite these fanatical Junglist pockets the rest of the country remained slow on the uptake. Manchester, still reeling from the crack wars which marked out the turn of the decade, was running scared of anything which had any associations with the bad boy lifestyle. Although the Nia Centre in Hulme did provide a venue for early Jungle raves, it wasn't until the more acceptable face of Drum 'n' Bass filtered through that the city centre clubs dared to represent the sound.

Despite a general lack of interest from the wider clubbing public, areas like Newcastle and Middlesbrough have built up small but similarly fanatical scenes. 'Jungle took a long time to catch on in this area,' explains Alan Clarke of Newcastle artists Elementz of Noize. 'A big reason for this is the fact that there isn't a big black population in Newcastle. You know what I mean? We're lucky because we got into it right from the start.'

Indeed both Alan and his brother Justin have championed the sound from the off, with their DJing slots at irregular club nights called 'Rinse', whilst also playing Techstep sounds every Thursday at the Barcode since early 1995.

Perhaps best known for its Handbag House clubs, the local Jungle/

Drum 'n' Bass scene had to take on the DIY ethos of the warehouse days with many of the parties being organised in makeshift venues like the arches of Newcastle's Byker Bridge. The Telegraph pub just around the corner from the city's main railway station opened its doors to a weekly event run by a loose collection known as OCP (Off Centre Productions) in 1995, soon becoming the essential meeting place for the scene. Run by local Drum 'n' Bass heads Hidden Agenda (whose releases on Metalheads offered superb examples of soulful stepping Breakbeat), Mr Foster and Covert, OCP personally took on the task of opening up the north east to Drum 'n' Bass, by encouraging better known artists to play at the Telegraph (Doc Scott being one of the regulars) or by promoting events like Goldie and the Metalheads at the Riverside.

Perhaps due to the successes of OCP, Rinse and the Byker Bridge parties, the Arena in neighbouring Middlesbrough opened its doors to Drum 'n' Bass in 1996. Called 'On It', these weekly events soon gained a reputation as being among the best in the country. Indeed the Metalheads crew described their 1996 Arena date as 'the best night of the tour'.

Meanwhile both the Midlands and East Anglia proved to be important breeding grounds for talent, much of which had been around since the Hardcore days. Along with DJ SS and his Formation and New Identity labels and Doc Scott's 31 Records, the Midlands became noted for artists like Essence of Aura, old skool Breakbeat technician Neil Trix and Carlito, whose 'Carlito's Way' single on Moving Shadow offered one of Jazzy Drum 'n' Bass's finest moments.

On the south east coast of Britain production teams like PFM led the way with their cool and haunting 'One and Only' on Bukem's Good Looking records, while E-Z Rollers and JMJ & Richie mixed the vibe with a Detroit Techno feel.

Moving Shadow took a step towards highlighting these artists from other regions with a series of compilation albums. Most of the other London tastemakers, however, tended to overlook anything outside the capital (with the obvious exception of Doc Scott). Indeed in an interview for *Muzik*, Fabio noted that he'd ignored a package sent to him by Newcastle's Hidden Agenda because of its north east origins. 'They sent me a DAT a couple of years ago, but when I saw it was from Newcastle I didn't bother to listen to it. I'm really bad, aren't I,' he admitted. 'And then, I lost the DAT anyway! So they sent me another and it was just unreal.'

Luckily Metalheads weren't put off by the artist's location and subsequently put out a series of highly acclaimed singles by the Geordies. Upon hearing the first Metalheads dub of 'Is It Love', however, Fabio instantly realised his mistake and set about commissioning a single for his Creative Source imprint.

Throughout the rest of England Drum 'n' Bass nights started to flourish in 1996, small clubs playing host to a selection of name DJs with unknown locals in support. However, the response of the larger clubs north of London was still a negative one. Only Cream in Liverpool took up the cause with any serious intent. It was a move which was to cause a minor tremor of dismay throughout the Drum 'n' Bass scene. The Cream night was to feature 'Logical Progressions' with L. T. J. Bukem as its resident, a move which was soon to call an end to Speed as Bukem decided to move on and concentrate on the alternative pastures offered by the House scene and its associated super clubs.

In a fit of despair which showed the scene's elitist tendencies in full, DJs, promoters and punters spoke out against the man. Increasingly being hailed a traitor, he soon became a focal point for a scene coming to terms with its own popularity. Reinforced's Dego McFarlane had a far more positive acceptance of the newcomers to the music. The new converts to Drum 'n' Bass might have only intended to stick around for as long as it was trendy, but he simply didn't care. He laughs:

When loads of new people first started coming in I just thought 'Oh well, welcome'. A lot of people reacted against it but they were keeping it from the people. I've already had a slating from the Rave times so I can deal with it. But some of these people hadn't ever experienced that before so they kept things to themselves by going, 'Man, there's all these people coming in. Where were they back in the day?' And I'd be like, 'I wasn't there when the first Jazz records came out but I still buy them'. I was happy that people were getting into the sound and if they're only into it for two weeks then OK. Thank you for listening for a while. I've spent years being on the underground when no one wanted to hear. Even people who were meant to be within the Drum 'n' Bass scene can't comprehend what it's like to be that underground for that long and be totally ignored by people. It doesn't matter if people only get into Drum 'n' Bass for a week, as long as they've tried then I think we should feel honoured.

Ironically the coupling of Bukem's 'Logical Progression' and Cream proved to be an unhappy one with Bukem walking before the end of the year. His reasons were that Cream wanted him to guarantee his appearance at the weekly Friday night event. Bukem wasn't prepared to do that, arguing that it was a 'Logical Progression' night, not a Bukem event.

If the growing popularity of Drum 'n' Bass presented a problem to some of the more elitist factors of the scene then for others it was a bonus for the years of hard work. Throughout 1995 London's bigger clubs made a commitment to Drum 'n' Bass. Most notable was south London's Ministry of Sound, which became the new monthly haunt for both Bukem's 'Logical Progression' and A.W.O.L.

With all the original DJs and MCs intact, the Ministry opened its doors to A.W.O.L. on Thursday 4 August, with the promoters unleashing a superb compilation album to coincide. By mid 1995 however the A.W.O.L. crew had moved base once more, subsequently taking up residency at London's SW1 club, a night which was described as 'the temple of boom' in *The Wire*.

The word of Jungle was further spread by the tours which started to emerge in 1995. Noted Jungle promoters Thunder and Joy took their show around the nation's clubs with a line up which included DJ Rap, Nicky Blackmarket, Micky Finn, Darren Jay and Brockie. A tour which proved to be a major success, it paved the way for similar tours by A.W.O.L. (who have since toured regularly), the Metalheads crew and of course Bukem's collective. All of whom took their respective versions to an ever wider audience, opening up the darkened corridors of the scene to newcomers everywhere.

RECOMMENDED LISTENING

'Parallel Minds' – 4 Hero (Reinforced)

'Black Secret Technology' – A Guy Called Gerald (Juiceox)

'Aquarius Rising' A Guy Called Gerald (Juicebox)

'So Far' – Alex Reece (Island)

'Timeless' – Goldie (Ffrr)

'The Deepest Cut Vol 1' – Omni Trio (Moving Shadow)

'The Haunted Science' – Omni Trio (Moving Shadow)

'Waveform' – T-Power (SOUR)

'Self Evident Truth of an Intuitive Mind' – T-Power (SOUR)

'68 Million Shades . . .' – Spring Heel Jack (Trade 2/Island)

'Versions' – Spring Heel Jack (Trade 2/Island)

'Balance of the Force' – Boymerang (Prototype)

'Emotions With Intellect' – Icons (Modern Urban Jazz)

'Dub Plate Selection Volume 1 – More Rockers (More Rockers)

'Live from Mars Vol 1' – Forces of Nature (Clean Up)

'Live from Mars Vol 2' – Forces of Nature (Clean Up)

'Dimensions of Sound' – EZ Rollers (Moving Shadow)

'Suspected' – Foul Play (Moving Shadow)

'Slow Motion' – J Majik (Infra Red)

'Thru The Haze' – Jaz Klash (Cup of Tea)

9: MUTANT REVISITED

DRUM 'N' BASS RETURNS TO THE DARKSIDE

Given the push-me-pull-me antics of Breakbeat creativity it was inevitable that the scene would rebel against the whole concept of Ambient. To a group of producers and DJs who had gone through the Hardcore and Dark eras this 'coffee table' strain of Drum 'n' Bass was little more than a diversion. The heart of Breakbeat for them had always been shrouded in darkness, its lifeblood the pursuit of the impossible. As a result, just as the Ambient sound had hit the mainstream in early 1995, many of its artists had already taken their music towards a new intensity where experimentation ruled supreme. A development which presented a double edged attack, it found the scene reinventing Dark by picking up the sounds of alienation – the ambience of dislocation – and taking them into the physical space of the dancefloor and the cerebral cortex of the mind.

At the forefront of this was the Metalheads label. Originally set up in the summer of 1994 to release Doc Scott and Goldie's collaborative effort 'Drumz VIP' which had been doing the rounds on dub plate since February of that year, Metalheads set out with a philosophy which, according to their press release, aimed to 'explore both the roots of Breakbeat and Jungle and rework it into a new dimension, Drum 'n' Bass'. Indeed Metalheads was to become the embodiment of the Drum 'n' Bass spirit of redefining the rules. Furthermore, by then the label had the bold aim of preserving the underground spirit of anarchy and adventure whilst also bridging the gap between underground music (and its inherent concerns) and commercialism. As such Metalheads made it clear that they wouldn't be happy aiming at the limited market of the scene's diehards; they wanted to take the word of Drum 'n' Bass to as many people as would listen.

Central to Metalheads, and indeed to this new version of Dark, was a pool of DJs and producers who worked under a variety of different names. People like Rupert Parkes, J Majik, Source Direct, Lemon D, Doc Scott, Hidden Agenda and of course Goldie. With an overriding love of Funk at the very core of the new darkness, the old Horrorcore samples had been replaced by foreboding strings while Breakbeats were cut up and layered into a series of bold yet brittle barrages of at times impenetrable grooves. The sound also embraced the original Jungle ideology of feeding off any other genre which came along.

In a sense, this latest move held the engineer and producer aloft as the real stars of the scene, as technical proficiency became increasingly revered. These people were no longer the raw scientists behind Hardcore; in fact they were now among the most skilled studio operators in the world. Their attitude towards the technology remained intent on pushing the hardware to its very extremes, and as such the subsequent music took on a fresh complexity, boasting of the producer's ingenious skill.

Rupert Parkes (aka Photek) and Source Direct achieved massive acclaim both with DJs and critics alike for their leftfield approach to Drum 'n' Bass. Quite at odds with the inner city stance of the Jungle front line, Parkes and Phil & Jim of Source Direct hailed from the middle class suburbia of St Albans. As such the standard association with inner city life was an aspect of Jungle's heritage to which neither could lay claim. However, what they brought to the equation was an experimental heritage referencing modern classical composers like Philip Glass and Stockhausen as much as the Industrial Funk scene of the 1980s. Their take on Jazz didn't encompass the usual introduction of a breezy horn refrain or piano motif appropriated from Jazz Funk; instead it echoed the free form intricacies and exact spaces of Byron Bowie's Art Ensemble of Chicago or 'On the Corner' era Miles Davis. Like Goldie, they also referenced a number of avant garde artists like David Sylvian, Brian Eno and Kraftwerk.

However, these musical influences rarely surfaced in their earlier incarnations with both Parkes's work as 'Aquarius' on Bukem's Good

Looking label and Source Direct's formative releases as 'Sounds of Life' on Certificate 18 displaying some of the least inviting excesses of the Ambient/Jazz and Hardcore styles.

It's under their Photek and Source Direct names that these two production teams proved to be at their most interesting. Parkes explains:

I see what I make as a continuation of where Jazz left off, as if everything stopped in 1971 and came out again in 1996. If I had been born at a different time and was making music in those days I'd probably be making Jazz Fusion, but being born in 1972, and seeing as how Techno and House and Hip Hop have happened, I think that this is where Jazz Fusion is at now. I'm making an extension, just another branch. Rather than just putting a few samples on a drum machine and then on a Drum 'n' Bass track, I'm taking it a bit deeper in.

A part of the Photek approach to taking things a 'bit deeper in' took the form of constructing breaks rather than merely sampling them. Representing the point where the needs of the DJ are no longer important, Parkes's approach allowed him to direct the music far away from the dance-floor constraints of Drum 'n' Bass.

Similarly Source Direct took the Drum 'n' Bass ethos way beyond the simple cutting up of an Amen or Apache break. For them the rhythmical approach involved precision surgery, cutting up unrecognisable Breakbeats into a complete aberration of their original form. At times awe-inspiring, whilst at other times almost unlistenable, both Photek and Source Direct took the Drum 'n' Bass sound on a trip which was aeons away from the origins of Jungle.

Yet they were both accepted into the folds of the scene with open arms. Perhaps one reason was that Parkes was seen to have grown with the scene itself, undergoing many of the same changes even though he didn't necessarily have the same background. Similarly Source Direct provided a number of club floor favourites while developing hand in hand with the Drum 'n' Bass front line. It could also be said that the experimental approach of both parties still sat very much within the constraints of the genre: limitations constructed by those DJs and producers who decided which artist's tracks were to be played, who would be name-checked in interviews and who would be ignored. Indeed in a scene which initially purported to embrace the notion of creative freedom, it was increasingly only a certain few who controlled what got through to the forefront and what remained hidden away.

In moves which adopted similar aims as those of the committee, the Drum 'n' Bass cognoscenti managed to control many aspects of the media, developing a climate towards the end of 1995 and through 1996 which found much of the media scared of misrepresenting things once again. Nobody wanted to promote (or be seen promoting) the wrong artists again so the word of a few people became paramount. If Goldie, Bukem, Fabio, Grooverider, Randall, Doc Scott, etc. said the track was cool then it was OK to write about it.

Increasingly the self-styled gurus of the scene would control sectors of the media (and indeed the wider industry) keen to be seen as being 'down with the Junglists'. Myth became truth as the scene made use of their power, encouraging certain records, artists and labels to be hyped up. Not only displaying just how strong the DJs had become, it also reflected just how weak journalists and editors sometimes appeared to be when faced with the Drum 'n' Bass front line. It was a golden period for this crew: they'd realised many of their aims and now they were all courting major record labels.

Realising that they represented good copy for the dance papers they played the Jungle card close to their chests, almost denying the existence of any other Breakbeat form outside their own.

Of course it all made perfect business sense. By creating a situation where they controlled the level of information, the style and standard of the music and the direction things would take, they were effectively playing a game of microeconomics. 'They like to believe that they're playing a different game to the major record companies but they're not,' explains Marc Royal, going on to suggest that the picture of unity among the Drum 'n' Bass fraternity which has been presented to a gullible section of the press is not exactly honest:

They're all trying to take control. It's just some people who are saying that the scene should be unified, about top tunes and not about style. The others are busy splitting things up. If a tune is good it should be played regardless of whether it's Dark, Jump Up or whatever. No DJ should have the right to sanction what is played and what isn't. The DJs have got too powerful, basically, and it's at the expense of producers. I think there's been a great willingness on the part of majors to buy up the DJs thinking that they are the talents, when all that they do is hook up with a producer to do their work.

As such, producers like Photek and Source Direct along with J Majik and of course Rob Playford were ultimately needed by the DJs. Not all as talented in the studio as they were behind the decks, DJs would team up with producers to help with their own tracks. However, Royal also suggests that the DJs have kept the producers down by controlling the scene. 'There's a certain aspect of this scene which is known as the rinse,' he argues. 'Ninety per cent of the stuff that is coming out is shit and I believe what's happening here is that certain people are rinsing the scene by keeping the quality down so that people can keep up with it. If the top producers were allowed to push things forward you'd see a lot of things that are raved about being ignored because the production isn't actually up to scratch.'

These considerations have long affected Royal whose output as T-Power has been rejected by many of the Drum 'n' Bass scene's DJs. Even though Grooverider would often drop Royal's second single 'The Elemental' (SOUR), his subsequent releases were virtually ignored. Part of this may have been due to the wide popularity of 'Mutant Jazz' and perhaps, as Royal himself admits, it was because for a while 'you couldn't bob your head to his beats'. More likely, however, is that Royal's music has not only aimed at pushing the boundaries of Drum 'n' Bass beyond the accepted limitations, but it has also attempted to break down the existing DJ hegemony. Indeed these concerns were central to the creation of his second album 'Waveform'. He explains:

When I started on 'Waveform' I had to ask myself how I would define Drum 'n' Bass. I decided that it was too restrictive. There's a very definite framework which is dictated by the DJs. You can't go below 164 bpm and you can't really go above 170. It has to be in 4/4 time, it has to comply with their version of what a groove is at any one time. And then who you are

affiliated with will determine whether or not it's played. For example, any
Rollers stuff that I might have done would not get the same recognition that
Shy FX might get, simply because he's known to be down with that sound. So
it all starts to come down to this 'guilt by association' idea. Which has to be
creatively constricting.

Throughout 1996 many of the Drum 'n' Bass front line dictated that things would go Dark again. Although the more experimental edge encapsulated this darkness the DJ-led sound called for simplicity. Standing out was the arrival of Techstep.

A sound which was heralded by DJ Trace's 'Mutant Revisited', a radical reworking of T-Power's 'Mutant Jazz', Techstep explored a world of cyber-fuelled distortion. Metallic rolling breaks cut through in elongated passages where rhythms married a stunning complexity with a groove-bound simplicity. Melody was redundant in this development; in its place sat elongated drones and machinery hum. If ever there was a tune for the 'Terminator' cyborg to dance to it lay in the stony-faced, guillotine-edged precision of Techstep.

The killer feature was the bass line. Called the Reese bass following its appropriation from seminal House artist Kevin Reece Saunderson (aka Reece Project), the melody was a simple one note octave played from high to low, bursting through the breaks like an adrenaline rush. It was a euphoric, orgasmic explosion of distorted sub-bass which would surge across the dancefloor like a fireball. Occasionally the bass line would employ a simple three note melody, running alongside the repetitive breaks, opening up for the intricate drum rolls and hi-hat patterns. Techstep was the true Dark force, a meeting of technological experimentation and ultimate floor control.

If there was a reaction against the warmth of the Ambient sound of Bukem's 'Logical Progression' posse, then it was Techstep. 'I think Drum 'n' Bass in '95 was fucking elevator music,' argues Dave Stone. 'When Speed started to happen all you had were these long stretches of strings with a bit of a break underneath. If it wasn't necessarily white man's Jungle it was certainly middle class Jungle. It lost its roots.'

Unusually for a scene so keen to retain control over the perception of Drum 'n' Bass, the latest term Techstep was coined by a record company.

Even stranger was the fact that this company was Emotif, the experimental offshoot of SOUR Records, a label once totally rejected by the inner circle. Bringing together some of the finest moments of the sound they released a compilation called 'Techsteppin', a title which fitted the music perfectly. 'The first time I heard "Mutant Revisited" I was blown away by its intensity,' recalls Stone. 'It was like Techno sounds mixed with Hardstep so when we were thinking of a name for the compilation "Techsteppin" came up. It just seemed to fit.'

'Techsteppin' featured exclusive tracks by Doc Scott and Grooverider along with stuff licensed from Dee Jay Recordings, a label which had also been instrumental in shaping this sound. However, the most significant additions to the album were the tracks by DJ Trace, Ed Rush and Nico. The faces behind most of the releases on No U Turn Records, a label which came to the fore in 1996 after four years of producing classic hard floor fillers, their trademark was the ridiculously loud Techstep bass sound which would push the soundsystems in the plethora of smaller clubs to the very limit.

METALHEADZ – THE SUNDAY SESSIONS

If 1994 had represented the summer of the Jungle rave then 1996 was the year everyone went small again. Inspired by the success of Speed promoters, record labels and DJs started to abandon the uncomfortable surroundings of the large venues like Bagley's in King's Cross, London, and instead concentrated on keeping the vibe close. To some it was a move which smacked of elitism but to others it was the only option in order to breathe fresh creativity into the scene.

SOUR/Emotif instigated a night in conjunction with No U Turn in the unlikely surroundings of Embargos in Chelsea called Movement (which was to move to Bar Rhumba on Shaftesbury Avenue in 1997). A new night in the shape of PM Scientists opened in a sweaty basement on Farringdon Road, London, while the Groove Connection Agency took over Speed's Thursday night residency at the Mars Bar to open Tempo with Fabio still at the controls.

Many of these smaller club developments were inspired by Speed and its overwhelming success. However, where Speed had come to represent the increasingly standardised Jazz and Ambient sound the newer clubs were intent on setting the next agenda, a part of which was about stamping crew identity on a public consciousness. Perhaps the finest example of this was the next step from the Metalheads crew and their move into club promotion, which promoted the identity of the label hand in hand with the fashion, ideology, lifestyle and, of course, music.

In early 1996 Goldie and crew set up shop at London's Blue Note Club for a regular Sunday night session. A night which had immediate impact on the Drum 'n' Bass scene, it quickly became one of the most popular clubs in London.

Metalheadz was a weekly workout for the label's associated personalities. A sonic laboratory where the regular DJs would spin exclusive dub plates which were so up front that the regulars could gain a picture of what lay ahead. Like a musical Tardis, Drum 'n' Bass's own time machine, to walk down the steps of the Blue Note and into the basement bar was to check out the future.

At first visit the Blue Note was like an unending corridor. Perhaps the smokiest venue in the capital, its upstairs chill-out bar seemed continuously choked by a crush of punters and a thick fog of cigarette smoke. Walking downstairs, however, the first thing you were aware of was the pounding soundsystem. With speakers spread throughout the length of the basement bar the sound was almost terrifying. A thumping bass which you could feel vibrating your eye sockets, crisp treble cutting through the darkness, a rushing energy of sound which engulfed you as soon as you stepped on to the dancefloor.

And once on the floor you became similarly engulfed by the writhing mass of dancers all lost in a sea of Drum 'n' Bass. Unlike any other club night at the Blue Note at the time, the downstairs crush at Metalheadz was as tight from one end of the room to the other. A crush which would spill out into the corridor with people's heads nodding over the pinball table. If Speed had seemed electric, then Metalheadz was nuclear powered.

The crowd itself was like a coming together of all sorts. Japanese girls in their Northwave trainers bobbed with south London bad boys dressed to chill in Tommy Hilfiger's finest. Students jigged next to Björk lookalikes, Junglists pulsating alongside House chicks. Black, white, Asian and

Australasian, all corners of the globe shoehorned into one sweating mass of bodies. Above the small stage the Metalheadz graphics team projected images of the label's metallic skull morphing into various shapes, spinning and disappearing into oblivion.

Around the decks stood the front line: Grooverider, skyscraper huge and eyes shining; Doc Scott and Goldie, talking tales of b-boy instinct and bass addiction; Kemistry and Storm; Dillinja and J Majik grinning with the energy, heads nodding to the tremor of sounds. A world of noises cascading across each other, a solar system of ideas collapsing into each other – into one unified euphoric heartbeat while Cleveland Watkiss and Conrad MCd, telling tales of twenty-first century Soul music.

Metalheadz's Sunday Session was a resounding success; a standard for all clubs. A walk along the Darkside which displayed the Metalheadz vision to full effect. However, this wasn't enough for a label who were never noted for standing on one spot. Goldie, Cristian and the rest of the Metalheadz team wanted the club night to be so much more and that would require space. A venue move was on the cards. This could be seen to be letting down the regulars, the weekly faithful who sweated it out through hot and cold, thick and thicker.

The answer to the problem was found with the idea of opening a Saturday session. In autumn 1996 Metalheadz opened in the comparatively cavernous surroundings of the Leisure Lounge in central London. Opening a Drum 'n' Bass club on a Saturday night was a gamble. A venue of its size would require far more than the Sunday Session's crowd so it would need to attract a lot of passing trade. The question also arose as to whether the Sunday vibe would transpose to the new venue.

In the end, however, it kicked off with as much energy as the Blue Note nights. Acting as a magnet for out of towners looking for a Drum 'n' Bass fix, curious clubbers who'd found the Blue Note's crowded spaces too claustrophobic and a whole army of new faithful drawn in by this buzz of Darkcore 1996 style.

RECOMMENDED LISTENING

'The Hidden Camera' – Photek (Science)

'Ni-Ten-Ichi-Ryu' – Photek (Science)

'Two Masks/Black Domina' – Source Direct (Science)

'The Crane' – Source Direct (Source Direct)

'Urban Style Music' – Dillinja (Metalheads)

'Mothership' – Ed Rush and Nico (No U Turn)

'Dark Metal' – Rufige Kru (Metalheads)

'Mutant Revisited' – DJ Trace (SOUR/Emotif)

'Squadron' – DJ Trace and Nico (No U Turn)

'5 Miles High' – TMF (Saidon)

'The Sleeper' – Spider Net (No U Turn)

'Astral/Yes' – Elementz of Noize (Emotif)

'Headspace' – B.L.I.M. (Emotif)

'Biohazard' – Dazzle-T & Quicky (Emotif)

'Still' – Boymerang (Prototype)

'Going Gets Tuff' – Lemon D (Prototype)

'Subway' – Ed Rush (Prototype)

'Mechanics/Prisms' – Dom & Roland (31 Seconds)

'Shadow Boxing' – Nasty Habits (31 Seconds)

'Still Life/The Rain' – Photek (Razors Edge)

'Arabian Nights' – J Majik (Metalheads)

'Skylab' – Ed Rush (Metalheads)

'Technology' – Ed Rush & Nico (No U Turn)

10: THE WORLD IS A GHETTO

CELEBRITY, THE INTERNATIONAL GROWTH OF DRUM 'N' BASS AND THE JUMP UP REACTION

September 1996, Club Maniac Love, Tokyo, B.L.I.M., Elementz of Noize and the SOUR posse are working the wheels, throwing down sets of adrenalised Techstepping breaks, dropping their own Dark and raw plates alongside cuts from the likes of Ed Rush and Trace. The Tokyo Drum 'n' Bass scene soaks up the relentless onslaught of beats with relish as the huge soundsystem surges with sub-bass power. Ribs pound and vision blurs as the system is pushed to its limit, the crew look across the dancefloor at the mayhem that has ensued. Clearly loving the experience, huge grins spread across their faces as MC Det spits a series of Ragga licks, shouting a fierce machine gun stutter of rhymes. The venue is rocking like nothing the British crew has ever seen before. It's a full on, 200 per cent nuclear powered rinse out and the Japanese crowd can't get enough.

Martin James, **Backbeat Science**

The word of Junglism was quick to spread around the world. With crews like SOUR taking their show abroad as early as 1994 they quickly realised that the only way that this scene could grow would be to push it geographically as well as musically. Subsequently as the Jungle committee played its power games SOUR set about selling the power of Jungle to the world. Aiming high they went straight to America and Japan, the biggest markets of all, but above all the slowest to pick up on anything, so it was only natural that these territories were the ones that had to be hit first. And if SOUR were to have any hope of waking up the sleeping giants of the music industry in Japan and the USA they were going to have to . . . make some noise.

SOUR did just that. Putting together a crew of DJs, MCs and PAs they set about spreading some bass instinct. Dave Stone:

We've taken the whole sound worldwide in a way that the London Hardcore would have been proud of. We stuck our necks out at that time further than any of the majors or the committee. Everyone was playing safe whilst we, underfunded and underground, just went for it. It actually caused me a lot of financial trouble at first because the benefits aren't immediate. But we believed in the scene. We even took dancers with us to show people abroad how to dance to this stuff.

The first tours included Apache, Shy FX, MC Det and T-Power. It's a line up of which the SOUR team are justifiably proud – a real product of the British multiracial vibe. 'We had a real racial mix with us,' enthuses Vini Medley. 'It was one of the best moments of my life to be involved in pro-moting something like this to the rest of the world.'

It was a show of racial unity which helped inspire a number of Jungle club nights to open across the USA (mainly in San Francisco and New York) and Japan. SOUR's vision didn't go down well everywhere, however. Indeed one of the shows in Paris was stopped as the venue was tear-gassed by local kids. 'I'm not sure if it was simply racially motivated,' says Medley. 'Maybe it was just what these kids liked to do, but it was totally fucked up. Part of the problem lay in the fact that the kids didn't really know how to respond to Jungle. There hadn't been a tradition of it in Paris and although Hip Hop was huge, the Breakbeats of Jungle kind of broke down in translation.'

A couple of years later Paris could boast of a regular Jungle night called 'Jungle Fever', a superb label in the shape of Selector and a regular Jungle show on Radio Nova hosted by DJ Gilb-R. Behind much of this change was promoter and label manager Catherine Piault who completely believed in the power of Drum 'n' Bass to bring different races together. Inspired by the scenes she'd witnessed in London's Jungle and Drum 'n'

Bass clubs she set about opening the way for Jungle with Selector Records and a club focus in the centre of Paris in the shape of Jungle Fever. With residencies from Gilb-R, Phantasy and Otis (south London Junglists who went to Paris for a holiday and never came back again!), Jungle Fever proved to be a great success with the biggest racial mixture a Paris club had ever seen.

The rest of Europe told a similar story with Jungle clubs opening up everywhere thanks to regular appearances from the likes of A Guy Called Gerald, Rap and Fabio & Grooverider. In Zurich, Switzerland, Club Gothic hosted regular Drum 'n' Bass nights. Similarly in Barcelona, Moog 2000 became a regular haunt for fans of this British export. The same was true throughout Germany, Spain, Holland and even parts of Italy. And the spread of Jungle wasn't just confined to Europe with Breakbeat feasts cropping up in Australia, Singapore and Malaysia. And, according to Fabio, even New Zealand had fallen for the vibes. 'Groove goes there (New Zealand) every year, man,' explained Fabio in an interview in *Wax*, '. . . he's kind of built the whole thing up out there by himself, single-handed.'

With the continued hard work of the labels and DJs the rest of the world has continued to open up to Jungle, coming back with their own versions while thankfully not getting caught up in the politics which have so often marred the UK scene.

Perhaps the most notable Jungle track to be created outside the UK was by Japan's Tetsya Komoro whose 'Wow War Tonight' sold a staggering 1.9 million copies in its home territory. A lame version of the UK style, its success proved to be a one-off for Jungle in Japan. However, the more organised UK labels like Metalheadz, Reinforced and SOUR have continued to sell well in that territory. In 1997 Emotif (the experimental subsidiary of SOUR) released a superb slice of Techno-meets-Hardstep by Japanese artists Dazzle-T and Quicky. Called 'Biohazard' it proved that not only had Japan taken up the sound, but that it had immersed itself in it so deeply it had become fully conversant in its language. 'Biohazard' promised many great things to come.

In America the sound had steadily grown in popularity since the days when SOUR had first crossed the Atlantic. With Jungle strongholds in San Francisco, LA and New York the story may have looked healthy. But the struggle was a hard one for the Stateside Junglists. Despite having roots firmly based in the Breakbeats of Hip Hop, the New York b-boys proved to be slow to pick up on the UK version. However, among the Latino crews, already clued into the fast percussive beats of their own House music, Jungle grew more steadily. 'The Spanish kids will hip the black kids up. New York got introduced to everything, House, whatever, through Spanish kids,' explained New York's MC Panic to *Mixmag*'s 2 Fingas in 1996. However, in New York's premier Jungle club Konkrete Jungle with resident DJ Wally, the story was of a much wider racial mix than just the Latino crews. As 2 Fingers goes on to suggest: 'Konkrete Jungle is about half full on both floors and that New York attitude you hear so much about isn't there. Instead the youths, a broad multicultural mix if ever I saw one, are smoking their herb and having it when a Hip Hop inspired tune comes down the pike. The kids like their Jungle on the rough side, tear out tunes, Techstep, the Hardcore Drum 'n' Bass. The rinsing business.'

Not surprisingly the Hip Hop influenced Jump Up tunes of DJ Hype and his Ganja Kru of Pascal and DJ Zinc have done big business on the dancefloor of Konkrete Jungle. As have a number of the tracks on SOUR's Hip Hop-inspired collection 'Nu Skool Flava'.

On the West Coast, meanwhile, Jungle was picking up a much wider market. Suburban Base head honcho Dan Donnelly suggests that previously his only buyers were the college kids. 'When we had a Rave label, it was very white middle class, suburban college kids. This time around it's taken on a different perspective to the extent that the LA gangs have adopted it. They don't really call it Jungle, it's "Breakbeat" to them but they're into everything that's going on.'

American labels like Liquid Sky and Sm:)e gradually became actively involved in putting out Jungle and Drum 'n' Bass sounds while in San Francisco Techno imprint Reflective released a stunning album in the shape of Subtropic's 'Homebrew'. America's love of Drum 'n' Bass, it would seem, was on the up.

Inevitably the increased interest around the world meant that a number of companies were able to spread their wings. SOUR set up a New York office in 1996 while later that year Dan Donnelly's Suburban Base Records opened up a US subsidiary called Sub-Base. Similarly these labels, along with Metalheads, Reinforced and the more organised imprints have been able to do licensing deals in places as far afield as Brazil, Argentina, Mexico, Australasia, Europe and of course America and Japan.

All of which provided much needed extra capital for the labels, opened up new places for DJs to perform and ultimately strengthened the power base of the UK scene.

CROSSING OVER

If ever proof was needed to back up MC Moose's claim that 'Jungle is like malaria . . . contagious', it could clearly be seen to be spreading through-out the Techno and House world from around 1995. In a complete about-turn the very same people who had rejected Hardcore at the turn of the decade were now showing respect to Jungle. Or more to the point, they'd embraced Jungle's respectable offshoot, Drum 'n' Bass.

It was a move which upset many of the old skool Junglists who were still angry at the original rejection they'd suffered. However, it could be said that there was nothing new in the ongoing trading of sounds. Drum 'n' Bass artists like Alex Reece, Wax Doctor and DJ Pulse had a long history of employing House and Techno influences. The twisted rhythmical patterns of Techno auteurs Black Dog had influenced many of the scene's more experimental artists since the earliest days of Jungle. Indeed Fabio and Grooverider's claim that the House sounds of Strictly Rhythm and Nu Groove were all Jungle related, locating Drum 'n' Bass deep inside the history and family of House, took this notion even further. House and Techno, it would seem, had long been intertwined with the growth of Jungle and Drum 'n' Bass.

The Techno scene had also provided a number of tracks which Drum 'n' Bass had taken on board, sped up to 45rpm on their decks and then played out. Among these were Andrea Parker's 'Melodious Thunk' on Mo' Wax whose high speed version was a regular in the sets of Elementz of Noize.

The best known adoption of a tune, however, came in the shape of Carl Craig's 'Bug in a Bassbin' which became a standard in what seemed like everyone's sets throughout 1995. In turn the track's influence could be heard everywhere. Its combination of swinging double bass and rough Funk fired Breakbeat science labs everywhere for a fresh workout.

Inevitably, as more people checked out the Drum 'n' Bass scene so the influence became a two way thing. Bukem's policy of taking Drum 'n' Bass to House in 1996 clubs had a very positive response with Parisian House DJ Laurent Garnier, among many others, being inspired enough by what he was hearing to include a Drum 'n' Bass section in his sets. The Techno scene too had picked up on the programming intricacies and Funk vibes of the time stretched Breakbeat.

Among the first to be influenced by Drum 'n' Bass were the more experimental artists like Richard James (aka Aphex Twin, AFX, etc.) and Mike Paradinas who records as U-ziq and Jake Slazenger among others. While the main force of the Drum 'n' Bass inner clique rejected most of the offerings of artists from outside the scene, in many ways these sonic experimenters were subsequently able to explore Breakbeat science without restrictions. To them it was unimportant whether or not DJs played their music; the exploration of sound was paramount.

Aphex Twin's use of the Drum 'n' Bass foundation resulted in some of his most challenging work ever. His 1996 album 'Richard H. James' fused self-constructed Breakbeats which were cut up into fragmented loops of brittle triplets and sequences so complex as to be almost unlistenable.

Like Richard James, Mike Paradinas's excitement for the Drum 'n' Bass potential stretched back to a love of Hardcore. Indeed the first U-ziq recordings were perhaps far more inspired by the Breakbeat scene than by Techno. 'I was totally into Hardcore at college', explains Paradinas. 'I loved a lot of the early Breakbeat stuff, although a lot of it was rubbish as well. When I started making music I think I was trying to make a version of Hardcore, that's where all of my mad breaks came from. I wasn't really a Techno person because I just wasn't into, or aware of that Detroit scene.'

This love of Breakbeat found Paradinas exploring a fierce terrain of fractured sonics. For instance, on his 1996 album 'Das Ist Ein Groovy Beat, Ja?' as Jake Slazenger he co-opted Breakbeat manipulation into a series of bizarre sound juxtapositions, pulling Drum 'n' Bass into an arena where a completely different perspective ruled. The same was true of his 'Urmer Bile Trax EP' under the guise of U-ziq which was released in February 1997. An eight track EP, it placed deconstructed Breakbeats into an eclectic mix up of

Electro, soundtracks, kitsch TV themes and wayward electronica. The result was an intense barrage of epileptic grooves; its Breakbeats spat out at random. Probably Paradinas's most difficult work yet, the press copies went out with a PR description calling this U-ziq incarnation the sound of 'Drill 'n' Bass'. Never meant to be serious, the joke genre was immediately taken up by *NME* who ran a 'Drill 'n' Bass' special. 'It was just supposed to be a way of describing the record,' explains Paradinas. 'I certainly never meant to invent a genre.'

Luke Vibert offered a similarly experimental vision, drawing on some of the same concerns as Drum 'n' Bass. Indeed his Trip Hop material under the name Wagon Christ contained a similar density as Darkcore although the Breakbeats were somewhat slower. However, it was in his Plug guise that Vibert explored Drum 'n' Bass Breakbeat cut ups to full effect on his trio of singles for Rising High Records. Like Paradinas, Vibert's approach involved a juxtaposition of textures, sounds and genres which took Breakbeat to a far stranger extreme than had been witnessed in the Drum 'n' Bass scene. Indeed for Vibert much of the stuff coming out of the Drum 'n' Bass scene was far too formulaic, especially on the Ambient side of things: '. . . it's too boring for me. They're [the Drum 'n' Bass scene] following rules. For a start you've got to make tracks so that Bukem can mix it nicely; start off with a nice introduction, so DJs can pick up the drumbeat.'

Vibert's album as Plug, 'Drum 'n' Bass for Papa', exaggerated this contempt for the DJ restriction on the artist by placing uncomfortable breaks alongside obscure music from the past. It was like an Easy Listening excursion which tugged your mind in a million directions, centred around an axis of Hip Hop experimentation. This approach to sound was also employed by Witchman on his 'Explorimenting Beats' album which echoed the Dark qualities of Hip Hop's Wu Tang Clan.

If these artists had appeared to be out on a limb with their sounds then Tom Jenkinson was almost on another planet. His Squarepusher material took the Breakbeat into outer space, combining sinuous Breakbeats with ambidextrous fretless bass. A sound which embraced such complexity that it completely entered the realm of head music. Here was the epitome of Breakbeat with the Funk taken out and replaced with a Jazz Fusion overload.

Despite some superbly audacious recordings the Drum 'n' Bass scene rejected most of these musicians out of hand. However, it would be wrong to suggest that all outsiders were cold shouldered. Ryz Maslen's Breakbeat explorations as Neotropic on Ntone were received exceptionally well among DJs as diverse as Grooverider and Alex Reece, who played out unmarked white labels of her '15 Levels of Magnification' mixes. Similarly, Techno artist Dave Harrow's Jazzy Drum 'n' Bass excursions as James Hardway on Recordings of Substance were openly revered, with Fabio regularly playing a dub of the 'Cool Jazz Mother Fucker EP'. This despite the fact that the beats were far more akin to the rigidity of Techno than the fluidity of Drum 'n' Bass. Also working in the Jazz area were House artists London Electricity whose rough breaks and wild sax solos ignited the audience at Middlesbrough's On It club as Peshay dropped a dub plate of 'Sister Stalking' on Hospital Records.

Perhaps the best known outsiders to be generally accepted, if not exactly revered, by the Drum 'n' Bass scene were East End Drum 'n' Bass surrealists Ashley Wales and John Coxon, aka Spring Heel Jack. From the very beginning the duo created a sound which concerned itself with the stylings of Drum 'n' Bass, yet stood apart from the beat science mainstream. Their first album 'There are Strings' combined lush orchestral sounds with washes of reverbed ambience and smooth Breakbeats. It was very much a product of its time, coming as it did during the Ambient rush of 1995. However, with their second album '68 Million Shades' they discovered a sound which was quite unlike any other Drum 'n' Bass of the time. Imbued with an obtuse sense of otherness, theirs was a sound which picked at the remnants of classical composition, flirted with tools of dub-version and juxtaposed brittle structures with luscious interludes. A music which was obsessively Dark yet split with shards of blinding light. Surrealist Drum 'n' Bass which, upon closer inspection, showed a basic energy which belied a love of the rougher styles of Jump Up, Hardstep and even Ragga. 'People hear the string arrangements and think that they're classical but they're not,' explains Ashley, himself a classically trained musician. 'The structures of the stuff on our tracks are simple structures which are arranged to sound complex.'

Spring Heel Jack's vision found a small level of success within the

Drum 'n' Bass scene even though Wales's and Coxon's sound was at odds with the style of the times, their arrangements unlike anyone else's. Perhaps a little too maverick for the demands of the dancefloor, they were nonetheless astounding. A fact which didn't go amiss with people on the edges of the scene. 'People get confused by this idea that there is some kind of a common, subconscious aim in all musicians, like we're all desperate to be a part of some little club,' suggests Coxon. 'But that's just bullshit. Everyone creates their own manifesto for what they're trying to achieve. People might then influence each other but to suggest that everyone is bound to one communal master plan is stupid.' 'No one's trying to be a part of a scene and if they are then it's a bit stupid really,' adds Wales. 'The best music comes first and the scene always follows.'

Spring Heel Jack may have already had a background in dance music, but very few musicians have made the Drum 'n' Bass transition from an entirely different genre. One artist who made a remarkable move, however, was Graham Sutton. Indeed so successful was his take on Drum 'n' Bass as Boymerang that he even recorded material for Grooverider's Prototype Label.

The strangest thing however is that Sutton hadn't come from the schools of Techno, House or even Trip Hop but from the unlikely area of Indie, albeit the experimental Indie sound of Bark Psychosis. For many of the scene's outsiders Boymerang's universal acceptance into the scene would probably come down to his initial adherence to the DJs' rules. This, however, would be doing Sutton's music a great disservice.

Bringing to bear both his love of sculptured sound and manipulated Breakbeats, Sutton successfully created a sound which was both his own and DJ-friendly. His first single 'Pro-Activ' on Leaf Records displayed a sharp understanding of the swing in some of the beats of Drum 'n' Bass. 'Getting Closer', the main track, took a haunting trumpet refrain and layered it over a rolling Soul step worthy of Omni Trio's Rob Haigh. So powerful a track in fact that it immediately became a regular at Speed, thus securing him a huge sense of respect within the scene.

In December 1996 Sutton compounded his position with a stunning single for Grooverider's Prototype Records. Called 'Still', it found Boymerang in much Darker terrain, his beats displaying the rigidity of

Techstep whilst an interwoven percussive break brought out a refreshing warmth. A sure fire Metalheads favourite Sutton followed the single up in April 1997 with 'Balance of the Force', a superb album presenting an astonishing combination of industrial experimentation and breaks which twisted in and out of each other like writhing serpents, intertwined yet separate.

THE MAINSTREAM CROSSOVER

Throughout 1996 the Drum 'n' Bass scene had to contend with its music hitting the mainstream in the most disturbing ways. Not through the Top of the Pops market place or even daytime radio, but through the unlikely channel of TV advertising. The sound of Drum 'n' Bass, so the advertisers thought, was the perfect accompaniment to soap commercials, shop ads and even soft drink promos. To add insult to injury the pop scene adopted Jungle in a new twist in the novelty single. Breakfast TV puppets Zig and Zag joked around to the 'Booyaka' single while middle aged and middle of the road disc jockey Terry Wogan adopted Breakbeats for his ridiculous Christmas single 'Jungle Bells'.

Without realising it Drum 'n' Bass had become a household sound, working its way into the public's subconscious alongside the brand names advertised. A bizarre twist for a scene which had produced a sound which had been ignored for years. Even stranger, however, was the speed with which the adverts made Drum 'n' Bass seem normal to the untutored ear.

Even though the reality was that these tracks were merely substandard versions which displayed none of the programming skill of real Drum 'n' Bass the irony was that they drew more people in. House fans who had previously complained that it all sounded the same were now getting used to the timestretched Breakbeats; slowly they were opening up to the scene's smoother sounds.

It was as though Drum 'n' Bass had become completely displaced from its formative roots. It had turned into the total antithesis to Jungle. Of course in the darkened rooms of the Blue Note, the sound was as cutting edge as ever, but in the outside world Bukem's 'Logical Progressions' compilation and to a lesser extent Goldie's 'Timeless' album had become the essential soundtracks for wine bar posers. The theme pubs of the country's cities would belt out their token Drum 'n' Bass CDs alongside Blur and Oasis.

Also essential to the collection was Everything But The Girl's 'Walking Wounded', ironically an album which possibly did more than any other to take Drum 'n' Bass into the heartland of the mainstream. Eschewing their reputation for guitar strumming bedsit angst, Everything But The Girl went through something of a rebirth in 1996, discovering Breakbeat science along the way. Scoring a top twenty hit with the album's Spring Heel Jack-produced title track, the duo also managed to cross their tracks over to the Drum 'n' Bass clubs thanks to their choice of remixers. Omni Trio reworked 'Walking Wounded' while in 1997 'Before Today' was reworked to startling effect by Adam F. Inevitably Everything But The Girl were written off as no hopers jumping on the Drum 'n' Bass bandwagon, and despite songwriter Ben Watt's obvious love of the sound the duo merely turned Drum 'n' Bass into music for hairdressing salons.

In late 1996 word reached the scene that David Bowie was also looking toward introducing Drum 'n' Bass into his vocabulary. Indeed he had already hinted at it with a one minute musical insert on his 1995 album 'I. Outside'. However, with his next project his sights seemed to be set on involving some of the scene's big guns.

To many of the older players in the scene this latest move by Bowie came as no surprise. As an artist keen to keep up with the latest developments in music's avant garde he'd constantly included cutting edge references in his tracks. Furthermore his Ambient excursion in 1977, 'Low', was heavily sampled throughout Hardcore and Dark, its moody vibes proving perfect for the scene at the time.

In November 1996 David Bowie released what seemed to be a collaboration with A Guy Called Gerald in the shape of 'Telling Lies'. Close inspection proved that it was in fact a remix package which featured both Gerald and Adam F. Bowie, it would seem, wasn't so keen to collaborate rather than use the scene to give his own work some street kudos. The scene, critics and even Bowie fans were scathing about it.

In February 1997 however Bowie finally released his own so-called Jungle single 'Little Wonder'. In the event it proved to be more an exercise in combining timestretched breakbeats with Glam Rock. It sounded like prime Bowie, taking influences as he had always done rather than simply stealing ideas.

However, Bowie's interest in the scene showed just how far things had come since the first shout of 'Hardcore, you know the score'. Jungle was now a household sound, albeit in a sanitised version. Within the scene itself celebrity status had been fast encroaching since Goldie's face was first plastered over the pages of every magazine and newspaper imaginable.

CELEBRITY

The greater acceptance of Drum 'n' Bass brought with it the inevitable search for the scene's stars. With his bleached and sculpted hair and gold teeth Goldie was an obvious choice and the media soon started to print the stories which surrounded him rather than simply cover his musical exploits. Very quickly Goldie started to take on celebrity status, his face adorning the front covers of papers and magazines for the latter half of 1995 and throughout the following year.

Music soon became secondary to this figure who seemed to be perfect for good stories. Even the dance magazines increasingly concentrated on the intrigues which surrounded the man.

An early example of this came with a much publicised fight between Goldie and Alex Reece. Reece wanted to use his Metalheads classic 'Pulp Fiction' on his debut album, but Goldie wanted to keep the track for his own Metalheads compilation 'Platinum Breaks'. Having proven to be the label's highest selling track, the long since deleted 'Pulp Fiction' would naturally be a prime selling point for the Metalheads compilation album. Reece on the other hand felt that the track belonged to him and subsequently wanted it for inclusion on his own album 'So Far'.

The argument that ensued spilled over into the public arena as the two allegedly fought it out in a club while magazine interviews offered perfect arenas for mud slinging. Naturally the press loved it. 'I don't want to slag the guy off, 'cos his own record's good,' complained Reece to *Select* at the time. 'But he's been slagging me off in all these magazines calling me a money grabber, and I just think, "Fucking hell, you owe me about twenty grand!"'

In the end Metalheads kept the original track while Reece recorded a totally different version entitled 'Pulp Friction'. Not only was it a sign of disharmony within the Metalheads camp but it also showed the media's lust for digging the dirt.

Another example of this was an episode on a British Airways flight to Germany which resulted in Goldie being escorted off the plane and being banned from ever using the company in future. The reason for this altercation? Goldie's alleged insistence on using his mobile phone whilst on board the plane, against the rules and conditions of air flight. 'I didn't know it was dangerous to bring phones on planes,' he said to *Time Out*. 'And in any case, why the fuck are they letting me bring it on board if it's dangerous? Isn't that the point of all those expensive X-ray machines?' Going into more detail about the incident Goldie continues:

Well, I had me mate chatting away in one ear and the steward telling me off in the other. By the time I've turned the thing off, the pilot's making an announcement on the intercom . . . 'There will be a delay of fifty minutes due to the inconsiderate behaviour of one of our passengers. At a cost of several thousands of pounds, we will have to turn the aircraft back to the terminal, where police are waiting to escort the passenger off the plane.' I just got up out of my chair and said to everyone, 'It's me he's fucking talking about, all right? Anyone got a fucking problem with that, they can talk to me. GOT IT?'

Inevitably the tabloids picked up on the story with delight, Goldie's reputation as a creative talent being reduced to the level of street hoodlum in a series of shocked news items. Increasingly even the smallest snippet of Goldie news became print-worthy. Indeed *NME* even printed a news piece about Goldie being taken to hospital following an allergic reaction to seafood. 'I had a Thai meal but I didn't realise it contained shrimps,' explained Goldie. 'I was roasting, I went red all over and I just told my manager to get me to a hospital fast. It was lucky I got there in time.'

However, the interest in this paled into insignificance next to the media frenzy which surrounded Goldie's relationship with pop star Björk. The couple became the favoured topic of gossip for months with their separate faces even gracing alternative covers of the same issue of *iD* magazine. Called the 'Love Issue', the inclusion of Goldie and Björk was a sensational promotion of the celebrity status of their relationship. The media buzzed about the on/off nature of Goldie and Björk's involvement with each other, with *Muzik* even announcing the couple's plans for marriage whilst other papers concentrated on Goldie's bust ups with Björk's ex-lover Tricky.

In a show of complete togetherness Goldie turned up at that year's MTV awards to hand over Björk's trophy to her. With their obvious mutual affection being beamed across the globe Goldie and Björk were now seen as an item everywhere. Indeed in a frightening twist one fan was so incensed at Björk's new found partner that he sent the Icelandic singer a letter bomb. The relationship soon cooled off with the couple seemingly paying the price of fame. The media, however, still remained obsessed with Goldie's private life.

As Goldie's relationship with Björk was at the height of media interest another very publicised altercation came in the shape of a slanging match with Keith Flint from The Prodigy. In an interview with *NME* Keith allegedly suggested that Goldie and Björk were 'corrupted by TV' and that they acted like prima donna 'arseholes' as if they were 'Michael Jackson and Lisa Marie Presley'. Goldie and Björk were incensed and in retaliation Goldie went on stage at Brighton's Essential Festival in May 1996 wearing a T-shirt with a picture of Keith emblazoned across it and the legend 'Cunt Face' written in bold letters.

The media jumped on it, printing stories of an ongoing battle between the two. However, in their Christmas 1996 issue *Muzik* brought the two together to kiss and make up in public. 'At first, when Keith tried to call me, I couldn't fucking speak to him, man,' Goldie exclaims. 'I was livid. I was going to send the boys round to his house . . . Grooverider wanted to punch his teeth out, Fabio wanted to kneecap him. All these people wanted to fuck him up because we all have history. It's total disrespect on his part, man. It was like, he can go on TV and be famous, but I can't because I'm from the street.'

The two may have patched things up but the episode told a much wider story. It was yet another example of Goldie's very public persona, a celebrity status which had much greater repercussions. Not only had it enabled him to become a household name, but as an ambassador of Drum 'n' Bass he opened up a lot of people to the scene.

On the other hand, however, others started putting down Goldie and his crew. They were accused of being nothing better than limelight grabbers who wanted to control everything. The inner core of the Drum 'n' Bass scene was increasingly portrayed by the Jump Up Jungle scene as acting like a mafia. To make matters worse Goldie had described Jungle as 'stupid music' on air during a debate on Kool FM's Sunday Forum. It was a statement which angered the fans of Jump Up who had stuck with the vibes of early 1994 despite the many directions the scene had since taken. Goldie and crew were increasingly held up as being responsible for the original split in the scene which resulted in the breakaway factions of Jungle and Drum 'n' Bass. However, these accusations were in many ways unfair. Indeed Dave Stone, someone who has been equally active in both scenes, goes as far as to say that Goldie has done all of the various Breakbeat scenes untold good by his celebrity antics:

There's a lot of people at the moment [late 1996] dissing Goldie because he's run off with the scene or he's maybe not representing. To me, and I've got to say this, Goldie is the only person who has remained true to his camp. Got a major deal under the name Metalheads. A hundred thousand people bought his album so in turn a hundred thousand people own a Metalheads product which in turn promotes his artists. For the scene it's all about staying true to those people who have remained true to you. People like Reinforced and Goldie have taken things forward whether the scene has liked it or not.

If the Drum 'n' Bass crews had, as Stone points out, taken the scene forward then the Jungle crews weren't happy with where they'd taken it. Having been very much ignored, the media's attention was held by Bukem, Goldie, Fabio and Grooverider and their respective crews; the rougher Jump Up Jungle scene had developed a powerful alternative to the apparent mainstream leanings of Drum 'n' Bass. Indeed it could be said that the Junglists were spurred on in reaction to Goldie and co's media-friendly antics and mainstream accepted sounds and in reaction, by 1997, Jump Up Jungle was gaining popularity once more.

REEEEWWWWIND – THE REACTION

As 1996 drew to a close the Jungle scene was gearing up to stage its own backlash against the Drum 'n' Bass hegemony. Claiming that they were the only ones who'd stayed true to the aims of Jungle they continued to push the music they believed in. This was the Hip Hop inspired Jump Up scene created by Mike De Underground, Hype, Micky Finn, Jumping Jack Frost, Special K, Brockie and Kenny Ken. A scene which held a very different slant on the Jungle story. Not for them the much loved tales of Fabio and Grooverider's seminal sets at Rage, De Underground's story told of completely different figures making up the foundation stones of the scene: Mike De Underground, Hype, Cool Hand Flex and Randall.

Central to the Jump Up movement was East London's Stratford shop and label De Underground. Owned by Mike De Underground who set up the label in 1989 to release Lennie De Ice's classic 'We Are E', the label and shop continued to work the underground sound of Jungle, acting as a meeting place for the scene's leading figures.

Jump Up represented the raw end of the Breakbeat spectrum. Rough beats which rushed the air with a battery of hard noises and tearing vocals, it was a sound which had long been ridiculed by the Drum 'n' Bass fraternity.

In her article 'Why Does Everyone Ignore Jump Up Jungle?', Bethan Cole noted that the art of the Jump Up sound was not in the 'dreamy, coffee table Jazz melodies' of Drum 'n' Bass but in the beats themselves, 'in the way they combine high impact technology with fluid, sophisticated, yet tearin' rhythms, with supremely catchy little tunes'.

In an almost word perfect rerun of Dark, the media's lack of interest in Jungle had allowed the perfect space for Jump Up to grow unnoticed. The space even managed to help the scene lose the hangers on who had created all of the problems at the Jungle raves in the first place. The 'bad boy' element and drug wars which culminated in six people being stabbed at Moving Shadow's Christmas Day 'Equinox' rave in 1995 had long gone; in their place stood a highly motivated, business-sussed collective with the singular aim of pushing their personal version of the Jungle story, their own individual sound and their own personal perspectives on life.

Flying in the face of the Metalheads crew, this scene had remained relatively anonymous throughout the previous three years, preferring to let the pirates carry the message and their music do the talking. This scene had never relied on the media for exposure. With Hype's 'Ganja Kru EP' flying out of the shops to the tune of 45,000 sales it's fair to say that they never will. Alternatively, however, this Jump Up twist on the story of Jungle offered yet another version of the truth to be plundered in order for a different set of DJs, producers and promoters to take control.

RECOMMENDED LISTENING

'Equations' – Endemic Void (Language) LP

'Lamb' – Lamb (Fontana) LP

'Feed Me Weird Things' – Squarepusher (Warp) LP

'Hard Normal Daddy' – Squarepusher (Warp) LP

'Homebrew' – Subtropic (Reflective) LP

'Deeper, Smoother, Wider Shit' – James Hardway (Substance) LP

'Kaminari' – Kumo (Psychomat) LP

'Bubble and Squeak' – Tom Jenkinson (Worm Interface)

'Brother Ignoramus/Sister Stalking' – London Electricity

'Super Sharp Shooter EP' – The Ganja Kru (Parousia)

'World of Music' – Dred Bass (Back 2 Basics)

'Freestyle of Bass' – DJ Hype (Ganja Records)

'Chemicals' – Da Demolition (Strictly Underground)

'In Da Hood' – Remarc (Suburban Base)

'Raw Dogs Relik' – Dream Team (Suburban Base)

'What Kind of World' – Ascend & Ultravibe (Back 2 Basics)

'Rockvhile' – Onyx (Strictly Underground)

11: AQUARIUS RISING

THE FUTURE

People have got to stop all of the positioning to try and be the coolest. Who's been in it the longest, who's got the most firing dub plates. It shouldn't be about that any more. Now it's got to be about taking it to the next stage of having as many people in the world into the music as possible. That doesn't mean diluting it to the lowest common denominator and taking it backwards. It means taking it forwards so that people can understand it.

Dave Stone

So what does the future hold for Breakbeat science? Where to next for the Junglists? As we move into the next stage of Jungle/Drum 'n' Bass' development, how will it compare to the boundary surfing euphoria of its finest moments?

As I write this the scene is surrounded by negativity. Some people have suggested that the music simply isn't groundbreaking any more, but is stuck in a state of stasis. Others have proposed the very opposite, claiming that the music is progressing too fast for the public to keep up with it. The major record labels are increasingly suggesting that record sales simply don't match the hype, while a number of the scene's long time supporters within the media can be heard grumbling about the unprofessional, star-like behaviour and bad attitude which has apparently overtaken some of the biggest names.

Within the scene itself, beneath the surface of the united face, lies a growing atmosphere of bitter conflict. The Drum 'n' Bass crew ridicules the

Jump Up massive, the Techstep scene rejects the Ambient crowd. And so it goes on in a vicious circle of bitching, backstabbing and open disrespect which threatens the very fabric of the scene as the factions struggle for dominance.

If the years of belief, passion and sheer hard work have been vindicated by the increased popularity of Jungle/Drum 'n' Bass, then the reaction hasn't been a completely positive one as the Jungle family has increasingly fragmented into a multitude of smaller, self-sufficient units. The original unity has become fractured, bringing things down to the street level of crew against crew, a closed shop mentality which breeds elitism.

Elitism itself will ultimately suffocate the creativity of any given scene. It prevents new life germinating from within while denying any cross fertilisation with outside forces. Subsequently elitism becomes anti-evolution; an impotent force. Marc Royal argues:

A lot of people are calling themselves scientists although they're closing down the boundaries. If people were perhaps a little less elitist about things then the sound would push things forward. There are people who want to keep things controlled by saying that they're the only ones being true, keeping it real. But how can you keep it real and be elitist at the same time? It's a contradiction in terms. Elitism comes from the angle of economic control. It's all about profit, financial standing within the economic community. Artists' creativity always suffers from elitism, so how the fuck do you keep something real? From the moment people realised you could make money out of it the scene stopped being real.

As we move towards the end of the century a number of Breakbeat artists are creating some of the most challenging, diverse and uplifting music ever. They are lifting things way beyond the constraints of the dance-floor or a dictated style code and into a new dimension.

Manchester's A Guy Called Gerald has always defined his own rules of play rather than fit in with anyone else's. In October 1996 he took the Breakbeat into the hitherto untouched territory of classical music. In a piece co-written with Errolyn Warren he proved that the African tradition of rhythm can work in perfect harmony with the melodic tradition of European high art, while his own material has taken a turn down an exciting and original path which finds vocals being dissected along with beats, thus deconstructing the pop aesthetic.

Gerald isn't the only Breakbeat visionary with an eye to the possibilities of the future. Others have wandered down their own unique paths. In Bristol Roni Size and DJ Krust have stripped Jazz Step down to its most basic, yet complex form whilst opening new doors in the process. In London's East End, T-Power has dismantled the basic 4/4 core of the Breakbeat and rebuilt it in a series of challenging isolationist visions. In St Albans, Source Direct have pushed technology to its extreme edge with their unique sonic contortions whilst in Ipswich both Photek and Omni Trio are racing ahead on their own personal paths.

So many others are appearing over the horizon, each walking a unique road: Dillinja, Klute, Boymerang, Skycutter and Endemic Void; JLM Productions, Hidden Agenda, Stickleback, B.L.I.M. and DJ Kane: names new and old. The list just goes on.

The story is the same throughout the world as the sound has evolved into something which is far bigger than the London-centric crews. In artists like DJ Wally in New York, Megashira in Germany and X-Pensive in France the sound of Jungle has escaped London's inner city sonic laboratories, moved way beyond the scene. Its energy has spread worldwide as the UK Breakbeat has become so much more important than any single individual.

Over the course of writing *State of Bass*, through every interview and each scrap of research, one phrase kept coming up: 'If people lose interest tomorrow, we'll just go back underground', the bold statement of a style renegade, the Breakbeat scientist remaining 'true' to the scene. However, if going back underground means closing down the possibilities, this movement will become no more interesting than a record etched with silence.

If, as Spring Heel Jack's John Coxon noted at the beginning of *State of Bass*, 'This music is all about moving forward', then let the music move beyond the prejudices of its surroundings. The future of Jungle/Drum 'n' Bass doesn't lie with 'those in the know', neither does it sit in the laps of a fortunate few who happen to have been there since the beginning. The future is for those with the vision and the inspiration to carry the flame of creativity forwards into the unknown. Regardless of background.

Jungle, Drum 'n' Bass, Darkcore, Ragga, Artcore, Jazzy Jungle, Jazz Step, Hardstep, Techstep, Rollers and Jump Up. It all comes down to one thing in the end . . . THE BREAKBEAT.

SOURCE
MATERIAL

BOOKS

Altered State – Matthew Collin (Serpent's Tail)
Junglist – Two Fingers and James T. Kirk (Boxtree)
The Ravescene Handbook (Ravescene)
Straight Outta Bristol – Phil Johnson (Hodder & Stoughton)
What Kind of House Party is This? – Jonathan Fleming (MIY Publishing)
The New Beats – S. H. Fernando Jr. (Payback Press)

TELEVISION

MTV – Partyzone: X-Project, Goldie and General Levy.

CD ROM

Junglism (Zone UK)

VIDEO

Junglism (Zone UK)

FANZINES

KNOWLEDGE – Issues 1–12
ATMOSPHERE – Various issues

MAGAZINES AND NEWSPAPERS

'Sound of Blackness' – Simon Reynolds (*The Wire*)
'Bristol Responds to Bass' – Emma Warren (*Jockey Slut*)
'Rumble in the Jungle' – Rupert Howe (*Muzik*)

'Slipping into Dark' – Simon Reynolds (*The Wire*)

'No More Mr Nice Guy' – Bethan Cole (*Mixmag*)

'It's a Jungle Out There' – Simon Reynolds (*Melody Maker*)

'Welcome to the Jungle' – Simon Reynolds (*Melody Maker*)

'Concrete Island' – Chris Sharp (*The Lizard*)

'Gangsta Rave' – Simon Reynolds (*Vibe*)

'Concrete Jungle' – 2 Fingers (*Mixmag*)

'Electric Kingdom' – Chris Campion (*URB, USA*)

'The Summer of Jungle' – Tony Marcus (*The Face*)

'History' – Julie Khan (*True Magazine*)

'Techno Prisoners' – Tim Fielding (*Mixmag*)

'The Future Sound of Music' – feature (*iD*)

'Jungle Juice' – 2 Fingers (*Mixmag*)

'Is Jungle Too Ruff?' – Jane Headon (*Mixmag*)

'Why Does Everyone Ignore Jump Up Jungle?' – Bethan Cole (*Mixmag*)

'Jungle, Jungle. The Last Dance Underground' – Kudwo Eshun (*iD*)

'Jungle Takes Japan' – Dom Phillips (*Mixmag*)

'Disruptive Elements' – Rob Young (*The Wire*)

'Above the Treeline' – Simon Reynolds (*The Wire*)

'It's All Jungle' – Steve Wright (*Making Music*)

'Earthbeats' – Roger Brown (*The Mix*)

A Guy Called Gerald, Nubian Sound Systems – Peter Shapiro (*The Wire*)

L. T. J. Bukem, Out on a Good Thing – Bethan Cole (*Mixmag*)

L. T. J. Bukem, The Pacemaker – Calvin Bush (*Muzik*)

L. T. J. Bukem, feature – unknown (*True*)

Doc Scott, What's Up Doc? (*Carl Loben*)

Dillinja, Feature Profile – Julian Rolfe (*Wax*)

Fabio, Wrong Side of the Tracks – Calvin Bush (*Muzik*)

Fabio and Grooverider, feature profile – Julian Rolfe (*Wax*)

General Levy, I run Jungle . . .' – unknown (*The Face*)

Goldie, Golden Nuggets (*Time Out*)

Goldie, Untitled (*Vibe*)

Goldie, news (*NME*)

Goldie, Raging Bullion – David Stubbs (*Melody Maker*)

Goldie, feature – Tim Barr (*The Mix*)

Goldie, The War is Over – Tony Marcus (*Mixmag*)

Goldie, It Could Be A Jungle Out There – unknown (*Guardian*)

Goldie, Heavy Metal Soul – Raymond Leon Roker (*Urb USA*)

Goldie and Keith Flint, Peace Talks – Dave Fowler (*Muzik*)

Grooverider – Ticket to Ride – Rupert Howe (*Muzik*)

Plug, Plug in a Bassbin – Rob Young (*The Wire*)

Photek, Feature Profile – Gamall Award (*Generator*)

Photek, Camera Obscura – Rupert Howe (*Muzik*)

Photek, So Why Then is He Shrinking – Susan Masters (*Mixmag*)

Photek, In Camera – Dorian Lynskey (*True*)

DJ Rap, First lady demanding respect . . . – Bethan Cole (*iD*)

Alex Reece, Cue Feature – Andrew Harrison (*Select*)

Alex Reece, Feature Profile – Luke Howe (*Generator*)

Source Direct, Direct Beats – John Russell (*FM*)

Suburban Base USA, Label Profile – Rupert Howe (*Muzik*)

All other interviews by Martin James